Sing and Rejoice

Favorite Hymns in Large Print

William D. Auld

editor

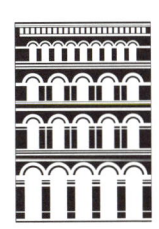

Westminster John Knox Press
Louisville, Kentucky

© 1997 William D. Auld

All rights reserved. No part of this book may be reproduced or transmitted in any form or by any means, electronic or mechanical, including photocopying, recording, or by any information storage or retrieval system, without permission in writing from the publisher. For information, address Westminster John Knox Press, 100 Witherspoon Street, Louisville, Kentucky 40202-1396.

Book design by A-R Editions, Madison, WI
Cover design by Alec Bartsch

First edition

Published by Westminster John Knox Press
Louisville, Kentucky

This book is printed on acid-free paper that meets the American National Standards Institute Z39.48 standard. ∞

PRINTED IN THE UNITED STATES OF AMERICA
97 98 99 00 01 02 03 04 05 — 10 9 8 7 6 5 4 3 2 1

ISBN 0-664-25712-7

Contents

Preface v

Worship

    Adoration and Praise 1

    Morning, Evening, and Closing 16

    Lord's Supper 25

    Advent, Christmas, and Epiphany 30

    Holy Week and Easter 46

    Pentecost and Holy Spirit 56

The Christian Life

    Discipleship 60

    Prayer 91

    Nature 103

The Church

    Fellowship 106

    Mission 110

Special Days

Thanksgiving 113

The Nation 116

Worship Aids 119

Indexes

Alphabetical Index of Tunes 243

Index of First Lines 247

Preface

This hymn collection is in response to a concern of an older resident of Mt. San Antonio Gardens Retirement Community in Pomona, California. "We need a new hymnal. The print is too small and the music keys are too high."

Not finding a large-print hymnal with the hymns preferred for worship and not finding enough hymns with lower keys, we created our own hymnal. Residents were involved in the selection of hymns, more comfortable musical keys, print type and size, and page size. We have attempted to meet the requirements of older people as they have expressed their needs to us.

The following served as guidelines:

> Large print for those with limited vision
> One hymn per page for those needing simplicity
> Broadly familiar hymns suitable for worship for persons from different denominations
> Comfortably pitched hymns for easier unison singing
> Traditional wording for those hymns most often memorized, and inclusive language where it seemed appropriate
> A finished product reasonable in size and weight

> Hymns in public domain not requiring copyright permissions
> Music pages with larger notation for easier playing

Since all the hymns included are traditional hymns of the church, most can be found in your hymnal. If your group prefers higher keys or a different hymn tune than the one chosen, you may use your own hymnals for accompaniment.

The inclusive language may be a problem for some users, but I believe that it will soon be expected by most residents of retirement and nursing homes, as local congregations increasingly use it. In most cases we followed the inclusive-language text of *The Presbyterian Hymnal* (1990).

I am grateful to the Revs. Douglas Edwards (Episcopal), Homer Henderson (United Church of Christ), Frank McCullough (American Baptist), John Najarian (Presbyterian), Roger Patterson (Lutheran—ECLA), and several retired church professionals living at Pilgrim Place, Claremont, California, for assistance in hymn selection; to Louis Ronfeldt and Gordon Winsor for help in choosing lower music keys; to Keith Snell, who used his keyboard and computer to lower music keys; to Ruth Auld and Carolyn Lyon for proofreading the text, and to the Religious Programs Committee of Mt. San Antonio Gardens for its guidance, encouragement, and support.

This hymnal is dedicated to the glory of God wherever it may be found useful. "With gratitude in your hearts sing psalms, hymns, and spiritual songs to God" (Colossians 3:16, NRSV).

WILLIAM D. AULD

Hymns

ADORATION AND PRAISE

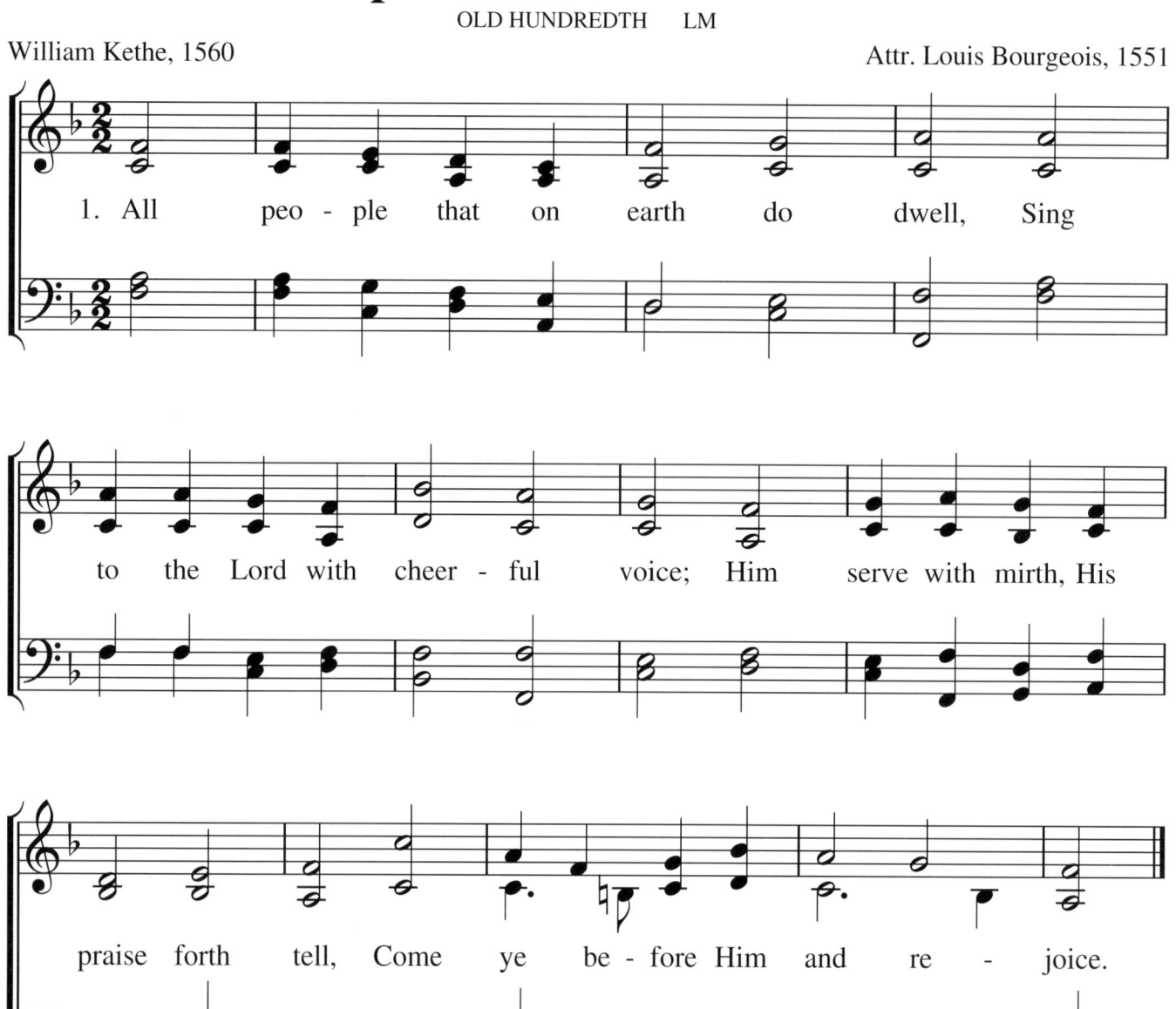

1 All People That on Earth Do Dwell

OLD HUNDREDTH   LM

William Kethe, 1560

Attr. Louis Bourgeois, 1551

1. All people that on earth do dwell, Sing to the Lord with cheerful voice; Him serve with mirth, His praise forth tell, Come ye before Him and rejoice.

ADORATION AND PRAISE

All People That on Earth Do Dwell   1

1. All people that on earth do dwell,
   Sing to the Lord with cheerful voice;
   Him serve with mirth, His praise forth tell,
   Come ye before Him and rejoice.

2. Know that the Lord is God indeed;
   Without our aid He did us make;
   We are His folk, He doth us feed,
   And for His sheep He doth us take.

3. O enter then His gates with praise,
   Approach with joy His courts unto;
   Praise, laud, and bless His name always,
   For it is seemly so to do.

4. For why? The Lord our God is good,
   His mercy is forever sure;
   His truth at all times firmly stood,
   And shall from age to age endure.

ADORATION AND PRAISE

2 Our God, Our Help in Ages Past
ST. ANNE   CM

Isaac Watts, 1719

William Croft, 1708

1. Our God, our help in ages past, Our hope for years to come, Our shelter from the stormy blast, And our eternal home.

Our God, Our Help in Ages Past

1. Our God, our help in ages past,
   Our hope for years to come,
   Our shelter from the stormy blast,
   And our eternal home.

2. Before the hills in order stood,
   Or earth received its frame,
   From everlasting Thou art God,
   To endless years the same.

3. A thousand ages in Thy sight
   Are like an evening gone;
   Short as the watch that ends the night
   Before the rising sun.

4. Time, like an ever-rolling stream,
   Soon bears us all away;
   We fly forgotten, as a dream
   Dies at the opening day.

5. Our God, our help in ages past,
   Our hope for years to come,
   Be Thou our guard while life shall last
   And our eternal home.

ADORATION AND PRAISE

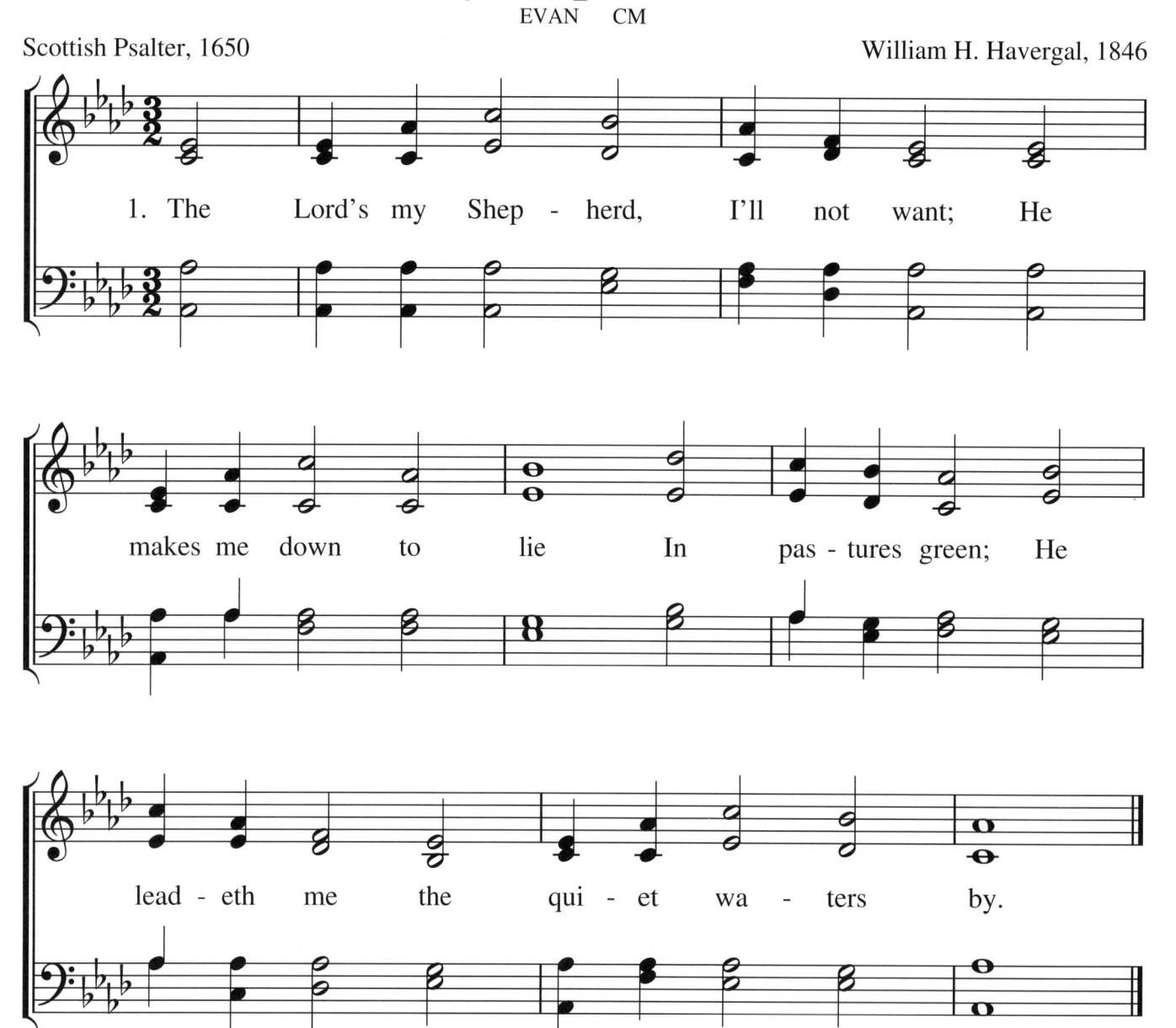

3 The Lord's My Shepherd, I'll Not Want

EVAN CM

Scottish Psalter, 1650 — William H. Havergal, 1846

1. The Lord's my Shepherd, I'll not want; He makes me down to lie In pastures green; He leadeth me the quiet waters by.

The Lord's My Shepherd, I'll Not Want

1. The Lord's my Shepherd, I'll not want;
   He makes me down to lie
   In pastures green; He leadeth me
   The quiet waters by.

2. My soul He doth restore again;
   And me to walk doth make
   Within the paths of righteousness,
   E'en for His own name's sake.

3. Yea, though I walk in death's dark vale,
   Yet will I fear none ill;
   For Thou art with me; and Thy rod
   And staff me comfort still.

4. My table Thou hast furnishèd
   In presence of my foes;
   My head Thou dost with oil anoint,
   And my cup overflows.

5. Goodness and mercy all my life
   Shall surely follow me;
   And in God's house forevermore
   My dwelling place shall be.

ADORATION AND PRAISE

4 Joyful, Joyful, We Adore Thee

HYMN TO JOY   8.7.8.7 D

Henry van Dyke, 1907; alt.   Ludwig van Beethoven, 1824

1. Joy-ful, joy-ful, we a-dore Thee, God of glo-ry, Lord of love;
Hearts un-fold like flowers be-fore Thee, Open-ing to the sun a-bove.
Melt the clouds of sin and sad-ness; Drive the dark of doubt a-way;
Giv-er of im-mor-tal glad-ness, Fill us with the light of day.

Joyful, Joyful, We Adore Thee

1. Joyful, joyful, we adore Thee,
   God of glory, Lord of love;
   Hearts unfold like flowers before Thee,
   Opening to the sun above.
   Melt the clouds of sin and sadness;
   Drive the dark of doubt away;
   Giver of immortal gladness,
   Fill us with the light of day.

2. All Thy works with joy surround Thee,
   Earth and heaven reflect Thy rays,
   Stars and angels sing around Thee,
   Center of unbroken praise.
   Field and forest, vale and mountain,
   Flowery meadow, flashing sea,
   Chanting bird and flowing fountain
   Call us to rejoice in Thee.

3. Mortals, join the happy chorus
   Which the morning stars began;
   Love divine is reigning o'er us,
   Joining all in heaven's plan.
   Ever singing, march we onward,
   Victors in the midst of strife;
   Joyful music leads us sunward
   In the triumph song of life.

ADORATION AND PRAISE

5 Holy, Holy, Holy! Lord God Almighty
NICAEA   11.12.12.10

Reginald Heber																			John B. Dykes, 1861

1. Holy, holy, holy! Lord God Almighty!
Early in the morning our song shall rise to Thee;
Holy, holy, holy! merciful and mighty!
God in three Persons, blessed Trinity!

ADORATION AND PRAISE

Holy, Holy, Holy! Lord God Almighty!   5

1. Holy, holy, holy! Lord God Almighty!
   Early in the morning our song shall rise to Thee;
   Holy, holy, holy! merciful and mighty!
   God in three Persons, blessed Trinity!

2. Holy, holy, holy! all the saints adore Thee,
   Casting down their golden crowns around the
     glassy sea;
   Cherubim and seraphim falling down before Thee,
   Who wert, and art, and evermore shalt be.

3. Holy, holy, holy! though the darkness hide Thee,
   Though the eye of sinfulness Thy glory may not see,
   Only Thou art holy; there is none beside Thee,
   Perfect in power, in love and purity.

4. Holy, holy, holy! Lord God Almighty!
   All Thy works shall praise Thy name, in earth and
     sky and sea;
   Holy, holy, holy! merciful and mighty!
   God in three Persons, blessed Trinity!

ADORATION AND PRAISE

6 O Worship the King, All Glorious Above
LYONS 10.10.11.11

Robert Grant, 1833; alt.
Attr. Johann Michael Haydn (1737–1806)

1. O worship the King, all glorious above! O gratefully sing God's power and God's love; Our shield and defender, the Ancient of Days, Pavilioned in splendor and girded with praise.

O Worship the King, All Glorious Above

1. O worship the King, all glorious above!
   O gratefully sing God's power and God's love;
   Our shield and defender, the Ancient of Days,
   Pavilioned in splendor and girded with praise.

2. O tell of God's might, O sing of God's grace,
   Whose robe is the light, whose canopy space.
   The chariots of heaven the deep thunderclouds form,
   And bright is God's path on the wings of the storm.

3. Thy bountiful care what tongue can recite?
   It breathes in the air, it shines in the light;
   It streams from the hills, it descends to the plain,
   And sweetly distills in the dew and the rain.

4. Frail children of dust, and feeble as frail,
   In Thee do we trust, nor find Thee to fail;
   Thy mercies how tender, how firm to the end,
   Our maker, defender, redeemer, and friend.

ADORATION AND PRAISE

7 Come, Thou Almighty King

ITALIAN HYMN 6.6.4.6.6.6.4

Collection of Hymns for Social Worship, 1757; alt. Felice de Giardini, 1769

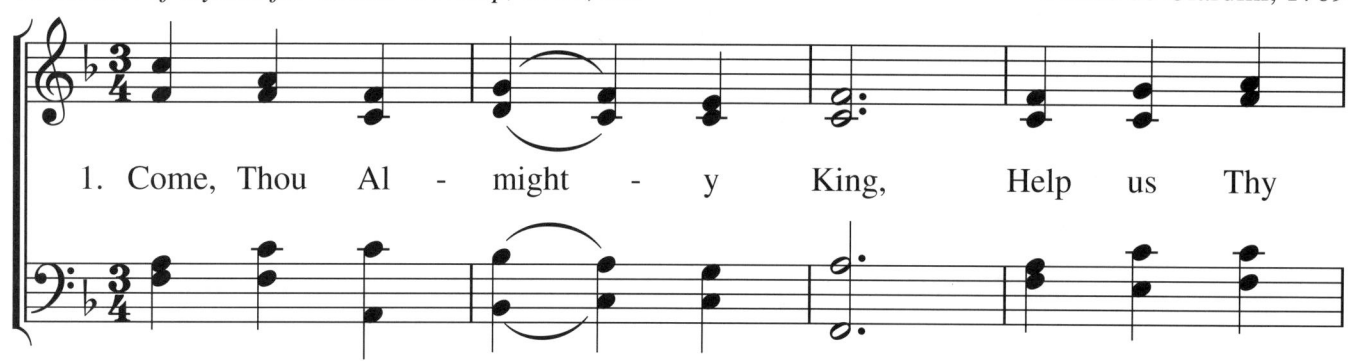

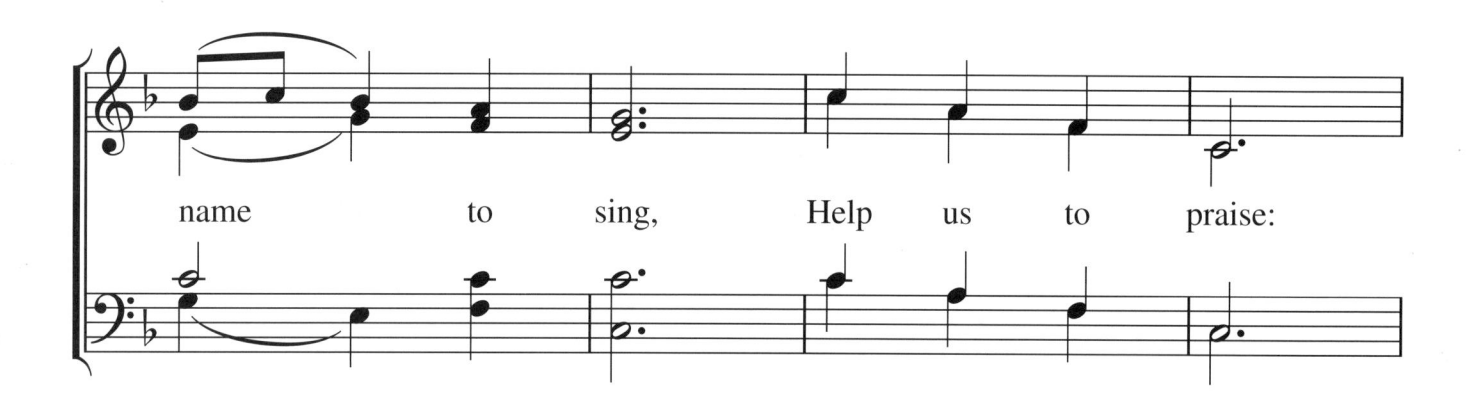

1. Come, Thou Almighty King, Help us Thy name to sing, Help us to praise: Father, all glorious, O'er all victorious, Come, and reign over us, Ancient of Days.

Come, Thou Almighty King

1. Come, Thou Almighty King,
   Help us Thy name to sing,
   Help us to praise:
   Father, all glorious,
   O'er all victorious,
   Come and reign over us, Ancient of Days.

2. Come, Thou Incarnate Word,
   Gird on Thy mighty sword.
   Our prayer attend:
   Come, and Thy people bless,
   And give Thy word success;
   Spirit of holiness, On us descend.

3. Come, Holy Comforter,
   Thy sacred witness bear,
   In this glad hour:
   Thou who almighty art,
   Now rule in every heart,
   And ne'er from us depart, Spirit of power.

4. To Thee, great One in Three,
   The highest praises be,
   Hence evermore!
   Thy sovereign majesty
   May we in glory see,
   And to eternity Love and adore.

ADORATION AND PRAISE

8 All Hail the Power of Jesus' Name
CORONATION   8.6.8.6.8.6

Edward Perronet, 1779 — Oliver Holden, 1793

1. All hail the power of Jesus' name! Let angels prostrate fall; Bring forth the royal diadem, And crown Him Lord of all! Bring forth the royal diadem, And crown Him Lord of all!

ADORATION AND PRAISE

All Hail the Power of Jesus' Name

8

1. All hail the power of Jesus' name!
   Let angels prostrate fall;
   Bring forth the royal diadem,
   And crown Him Lord of all!
   Bring forth the royal diadem,
   And crown Him Lord of all!

2. Ye chosen seed of Israel's race,
   Ye ransomed from the fall,
   Hail Him who saves you by His grace,
   And crown Him Lord of all!
   Hail Him who saves you by His grace,
   And crown Him Lord of all!

3. Let every kindred, every tribe,
   On this terrestrial ball,
   To Him all majesty ascribe,
   And crown Him Lord of all!
   To Him all majesty ascribe,
   And crown Him Lord of all!

4. O that with yonder sacred throng
   We at His feet may fall!
   We'll join the everlasting song,
   And crown Him Lord of all!
   We'll join the everlasting song,
   And crown Him Lord of all!

ADORATION AND PRAISE

9 Praise Ye the Lord, the Almighty

LOBE DEN HERREN   14.14.4.7.8

Joachim Neander, 1680
Trans. by Catherine Winkworth, 1863

Stralsund *Ernewerten Gesangbuch,* 1665
Harm. *The Chorale Book for England,* 1863

1. Praise ye the Lord, the Almighty, the King of creation! O my soul, praise Him, for He is thy health and salvation! All ye who hear, Now to His temple draw near; Join me in glad adoration!

Praise Ye the Lord, the Almighty

1. Praise ye the Lord, the Almighty,
   The King of creation!
   O my soul, praise Him,
   For He is thy health and salvation!
   All ye who hear,
   Now to His temple draw near;
   Join me in glad adoration!

2. Praise ye the Lord, who o'er all things
   So wondrously reigneth,
   Shelters thee under His wings,
   Yea, so gently sustaineth!
   Hast thou not seen
   How thy desires e'er have been
   Granted in what He ordaineth?

3. Praise ye the Lord! O let all
   That is in me adore Him!
   All that hath life and breath,
   Come now with praises before Him!
   Let the amen
   Sound from His people again;
   Gladly for aye we adore Him.

ADORATION AND PRAISE

10 Rejoice, the Lord Is King
DARWALL'S 148TH   6.6.6.6.8.8

Charles Wesley, 1746   John Darwall, 1770

1. Rejoice, the Lord is King! Your Lord and King adore! Rejoice, give thanks, and sing, And triumph evermore: Lift up your heart, lift up your voice! Rejoice, again I say, rejoice!

Rejoice, the Lord Is King

ADORATION AND PRAISE

10

1. Rejoice, the Lord is King!
   Your Lord and King adore!
   Rejoice, give thanks, and sing,
   And triumph evermore:
      Lift up your heart,
      Lift up your voice!
      Rejoice, again I say, rejoice!

2. God's kingdom cannot fail,
   Christ rules o'er earth and heaven;
   The keys of death and hell
   Are to our Jesus given:
      Lift up your heart,
      Lift up your voice!
      Rejoice, again I say, rejoice!

3. Rejoice in glorious hope!
   For Christ, the Judge, shall come
   To glorify the saints
   For their eternal home:
      Lift up your heart,
      Lift up your voice!
      Rejoice, again I say, rejoice!

ADORATION AND PRAISE

11 O for a Thousand Tongues to Sing

AZMON CM

Charles Wesley, 1738

Carl G. Gläser, 1828
Arr. Lowell Mason, 1839

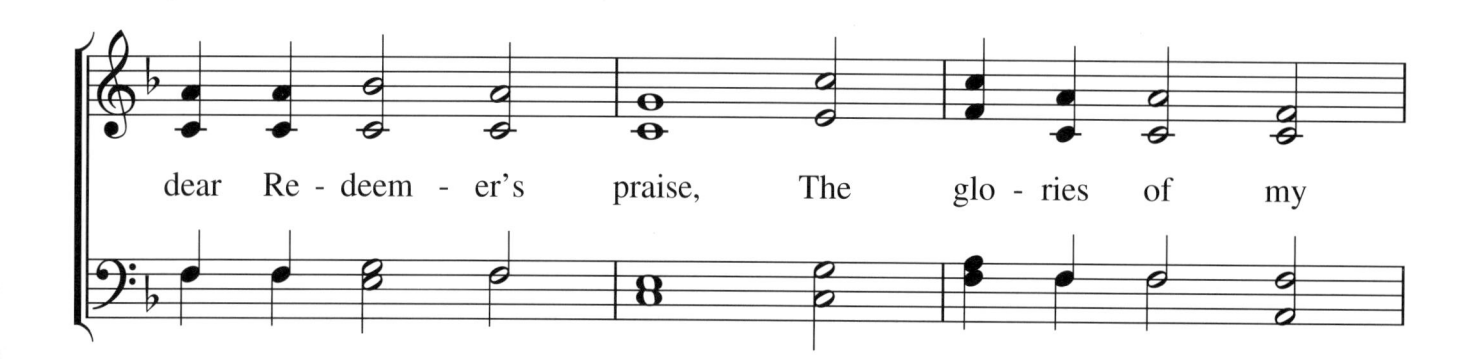

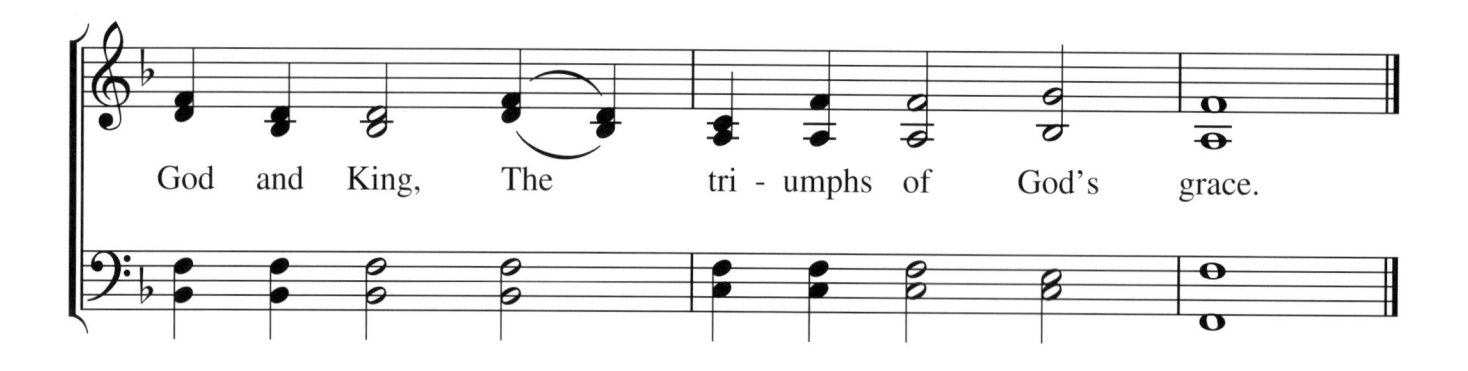

1. O for a thousand tongues to sing My dear Redeemer's praise, The glories of my God and King, The triumphs of God's grace.

O for a Thousand Tongues to Sing

1. O for a thousand tongues to sing
   My dear Redeemer's praise,
   The glories of my God and King,
   The triumphs of God's grace!

2. Jesus, the name that charms our fears,
   That bids our sorrows cease;
   'Tis music in the sinner's ears,
   'Tis life, and health, and peace.

3. Christ breaks the power of reigning sin,
   And sets the prisoner free;
   Christ's blood can make the sinful clean,
   Christ's blood availed for me.

4. My gracious Master and my God,
   Assist me to proclaim,
   To spread through all the earth abroad
   The honors of Thy name.

ADORATION AND PRAISE

12 Ye Servants of God, Your Master Proclaim

HANOVER 10.10.11.11

Charles Wesley, 1739

Attr. William Croft, 1708
A Supplement to the New Version of the Psalms, 1708

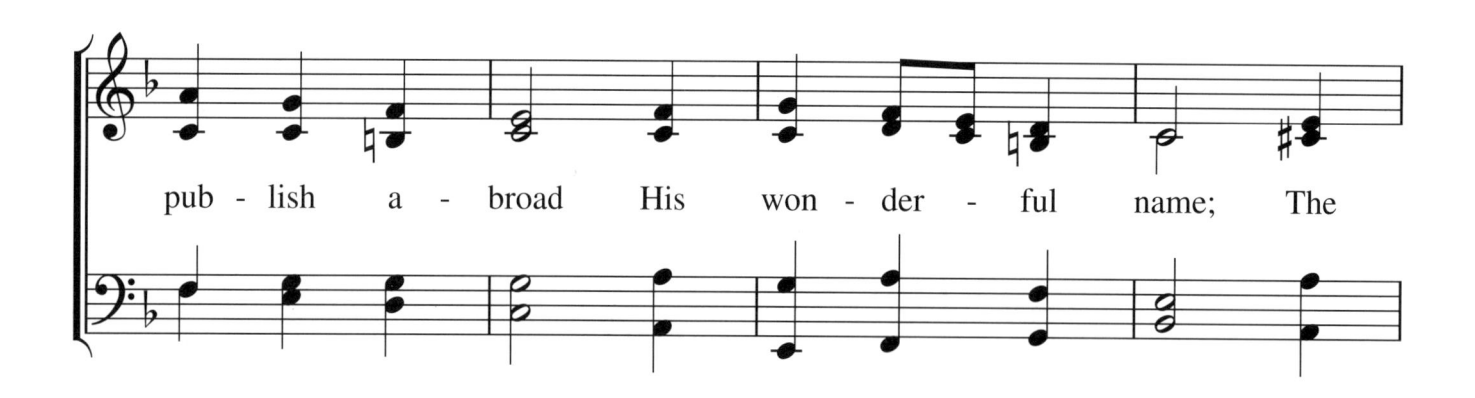

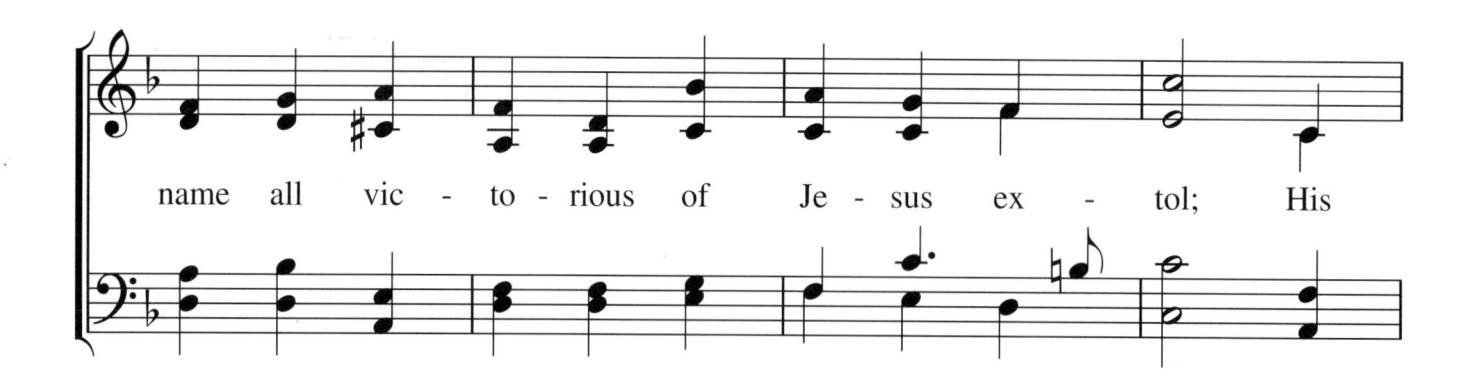

1. Ye servants of God, your Master proclaim, And publish abroad His wonderful name; The name all victorious of Jesus extol; His kingdom is glorious, He rules over all.

Ye Servants of God, Your Master Proclaim

1. Ye servants of God, your Master proclaim,
   And publish abroad His wonderful name;
   The name all victorious of Jesus extol;
   His kingdom is glorious, He rules over all.

2. God ruleth on high, almighty to save;
   And still He is nigh—His presence we have;
   The great congregation His triumph shall sing,
   Ascribing salvation to Jesus our King.

3. "Salvation to God, who sits on the throne,"
   Let all cry aloud, and honor the Son;
   The praises of Jesus the angels proclaim,
   Fall down on their faces, and worship the Lamb.

4. Then let us adore, and give Him His right,
   All glory and power, all wisdom and might,
   All honor and blessing, with angels above,
   And thanks never ceasing, and infinite love.

ADORATION AND PRAISE

13 Crown Him with Many Crowns
DIADEMATA   SMD

Matthew Bridges, 1851   George Job Elvey, 1868

1. Crown Him with many crowns, The Lamb upon His throne; Hark, how the heavenly anthem drowns All music but its own! Awake, my soul, and sing Of Him who died for thee, And hail Him as thy matchless King Through all eternity.

Crown Him with Many Crowns

1. Crown Him with many crowns,
   The Lamb upon His throne;
   Hark, how the heavenly anthem drowns
   All music but its own!
   Awake, my soul, and sing
   Of Him who died for thee,
   And hail Him as Thy matchless King
   Through all eternity.

2. Crown Him the Lord of love;
   Behold His hands and side,
   Rich wounds, yet visible above,
   In beauty glorified:
   No angel in the sky
   Can fully bear that sight,
   But downward bends his burning eye
   At mysteries so bright.

3. Crown Him the Lord of years,
   The Potentate of time;
   Creator of the rolling spheres,
   Ineffably sublime.
   All hail, Redeemer, hail!
   For Thou has died for me;
   Thy praise shall never, never fail
   Throughout eternity.

ADORATION AND PRAISE

14 Immortal, Invisible, God Only Wise
ST. DENIO 11.11.11.11

Walter Chalmers Smith, 1867

Welsh folk melody
Adapted in *Caniadau y Cyssegr,* 1839

1. Immortal, invisible, God only wise, In light inaccessible hid from our eyes, Most blessed, most glorious, the Ancient of Days, Almighty, victorious, Thy great name we praise.

Immortal, Invisible, God Only Wise

14

1. Immortal, invisible, God only wise,
   In light inaccessible hid from our eyes,
   Most blessed, most glorious, the Ancient of Days,
   Almighty, victorious, Thy great name we praise.

2. Unresting, unhasting, and silent as light,
   Nor wanting, nor wasting, Thou rulest in might;
   Thy justice like mountains high soaring above
   Thy clouds, which are fountains of goodness and love.

3. To all, life Thou givest, to both great and small;
   In all life Thou livest, the true life of all;
   We blossom and flourish like leaves on the tree,
   Then wither and perish; but naught changeth Thee.

4. Thou reignest in glory, Thou rulest in light,
   Thine angels adore Thee, all veiling their sight;
   All praise we would render; O help us to see
   'Tis only the splendor of light hideth Thee!

ADORATION AND PRAISE

15 A Mighty Fortress Is Our God
EIN' FESTE BURG   8.7.8.7.6.6.6.6.7

Martin Luther, 1529
Trans. Frederick Henry Hedge, 1852

Martin Luther, 1529

1. A might-y for-tress is our God, A bul-wark nev-er fail-ing; Our help-er He a-mid the flood Of mor-tal ills pre-vail-ing. For still our an-cient foe Doth seek to work us woe; His craft and power are great, And, armed with cru-el hate, On earth is not his e-qual.

A Mighty Fortress Is Our God

1. A mighty fortress is our God,
   A bulwark never failing;
   Our helper He amid the flood
   Of mortal ills prevailing.
   For still our ancient foe
   Doth seek to work us woe;
   His craft and power are great,
   And, armed with cruel hate,
   On earth is not his equal.

2. Did we in our own strength confide,
   Our striving would be losing;
   Were not the right Man on our side;
   The Man of God's own choosing,
   Dost ask who that may be?
   Christ Jesus, it is He,
   Lord Sabaoth His name,
   From age to age the same,
   And He must win the battle.

3. That word above all earthly powers,
   No thanks to them, abideth;
   The Spirit and the gifts are ours
   Through Him who with us sideth;
   Let goods and kindred go,
   This mortal life also;
   The body they may kill,
   God's truth abideth still,
   His kingdom is forever.

MORNING, EVENING, AND CLOSING

16 When Morning Gilds the Skies

LAUDES DOMINI   6.6.6 D

German Hymn, c. 1800
Trans. Edward Caswall, 1853, 1858; alt.

Joseph Barnby, 1868

1. When morning gilds the skies, my heart awaking cries: May Jesus Christ be praised! Alike at work and prayer To Jesus I repair: May Jesus Christ be praised!

When Morning Gilds the Skies

16

1. When morning gilds the skies,
   My heart awaking cries:
   May Jesus Christ be praised!
   Alike at work and prayer
   To Jesus I repair:
   May Jesus Christ be praised!

2. Does sadness fill my mind?
   A solace here I find:
   May Jesus Christ be praised!
   Or fades my earthly bliss?
   My comfort still is this:
   May Jesus Christ be praised!

3. Be this, while life is mine,
   My canticle divine:
   May Jesus Christ be praised!
   Be this the eternal song
   Through all the ages long:
   May Jesus Christ be praised!

MORNING, EVENING, AND CLOSING

17 All Praise to Thee, My God, This Night

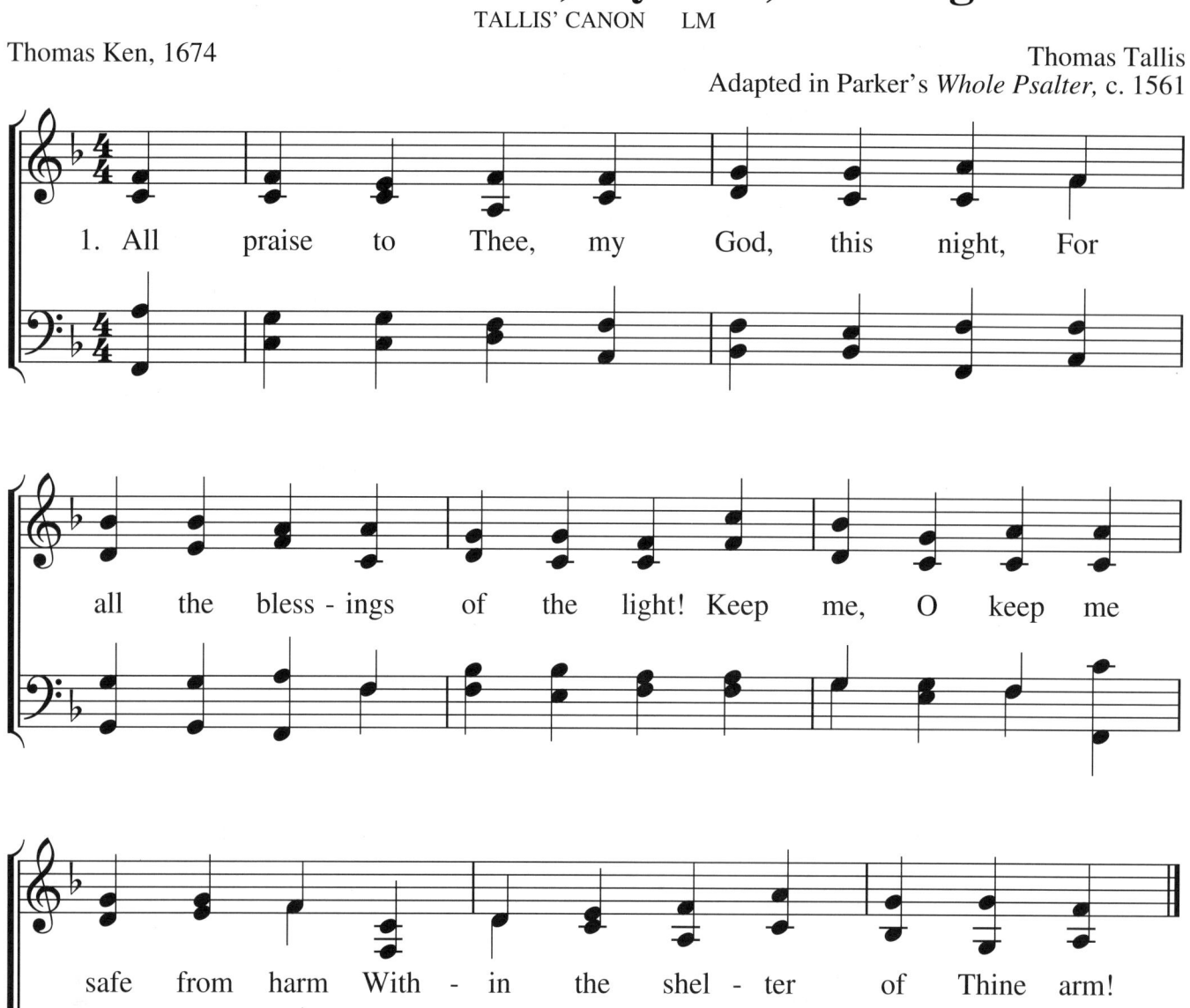

TALLIS' CANON LM

Thomas Ken, 1674

Thomas Tallis
Adapted in Parker's *Whole Psalter*, c. 1561

1. All praise to Thee, my God, this night, For all the bless-ings of the light! Keep me, O keep me safe from harm With-in the shel-ter of Thine arm!

All Praise to Thee, My God, This Night

1. All praise to Thee, my God, this night,
   For all the blessings of the light!
   Keep me, O keep me safe from harm
   Within the shelter of Thine arm!

2. Forgive me, Lord, through Christ, I pray,
   The wrong that I have done this day,
   That I, before I sleep, may be
   At peace with neighbor, self, and Thee.

3. O may my soul on Thee repose,
   And with sweet sleep mine eyelids close;
   Sleep that shall me more vigorous make
   To serve Thee, God, when I awake.

4. Praise God, from whom all blessings flow;
   Praise God, all creatures here below;
   Praise God above, ye heavenly host;
   Praise Father, Son, and Holy Ghost.

MORNING, EVENING, AND CLOSING

18 The Day Thou Gavest, Lord, Is Ended

ST. CLEMENT 9.8.9.8

John Ellerton, 1870

Clement Cottewill Scholefield, 1874

1. The day Thou gav-est, Lord, is end-ed, The dark-ness falls at Thy be-hest; To Thee our morn-ing hymns as-cend-ed, Thy praise shall hal-low now our rest.

The Day Thou Gavest, Lord, Is Ended

1. The day Thou gavest, Lord, is ended,
   The darkness falls at Thy behest;
   To Thee our morning hymns ascended,
   Thy praise shall hallow now our rest.

2. We thank Thee that Thy church unsleeping,
   While earth rolls onward into light,
   Through all the world a watch is keeping
   And rests not now by day or night.

3. As o'er each continent and island
   The dawn leads on another day,
   The voice of prayer is never silent,
   Nor dies the strain of praise away.

4. The sun that bids us rest is waking
   Thy children 'neath the western sky,
   And hour by hour fresh lips are making
   Thy wondrous doings heard on high.

5. So be it, Lord; Thy throne shall never,
   Like earth's proud empires, pass away;
   Thy kingdom stands, and grows forever
   Till all Thy creatures own Thy sway.

MORNING, EVENING, AND CLOSING

19 Day Is Dying in the West

EVENING PRAISE   7.7.7.7.4 with refrain

Mary A. Lathbury, 1877   William F. Sherwin, 1877

1. Day is dying in the west; Heaven is touching earth with rest: Wait and worship while the night Sets her evening lamps a-light Through all the sky.

Refrain

Holy, holy, holy, Lord God of Hosts! Heaven and earth are full of Thee! Heaven and earth are praising Thee, O Lord most high!

Day Is Dying in the West

1. Day is dying in the west;
   Heaven is touching earth with rest:
   Wait and worship while the night
   Sets her evening lamps alight
   Through all the sky.

   Refrain
   Holy, holy, holy! Lord God of Hosts!
   Heaven and earth are full of Thee!
   Heaven and earth are praising Thee,
   O Lord Most High!

2. Lord of life, beneath the dome
   Of the universe, Thy home,
   Gather us who seek Thy face
   To the fold of Thy embrace,
   For Thou art nigh.

   Refrain

3. When forever from our sight
   Pass the stars, the day, the night,
   Lord of angels, on our eyes
   Let eternal morning rise,
   And shadows end.

   Refrain

MORNING, EVENING, AND CLOSING

20 Sun of My Soul, Thou Savior Dear

HURSLEY LM

John Keble, 1820

Katholisches Gesangbuch,
Vienna, 1774

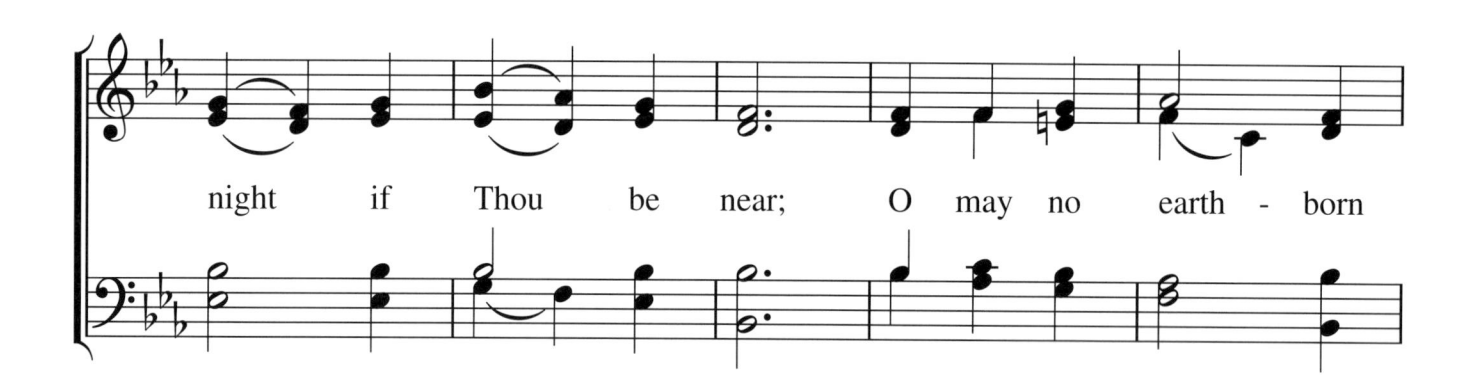

1. Sun of my soul, Thou Savior dear, It is not night if Thou be near; O may no earth-born cloud arise To hide Thee from Thy servant's eyes.

Sun of My Soul, Thou Savior Dear

1. Sun of my soul, Thou Savior dear,
   It is not night if Thou be near;
   O may no earthborn cloud arise
   To hide Thee from Thy servant's eyes.

2. When the soft dews of kindly sleep
   My wearied eyelids gently steep,
   Be my last thought, how sweet to rest
   Forever on my Savior's breast.

3. Abide with me from morn till eve,
   For without Thee I cannot live;
   Abide with me when night is nigh,
   For without Thee I dare not die.

4. Watch by the sick; enrich the poor
   With blessings from Thy boundless store;
   Be every mourner's sleep tonight,
   Like infants' slumbers, pure and light.

5. Come near and bless us when we wake,
   Ere through the world our way we take,
   Till in the ocean of Thy love,
   We lose ourselves in heaven above.

MORNING, EVENING, AND CLOSING

21 Abide with Me

EVENTIDE   10.10.10.10

Henry Francis Lyte, 1847

William Henry Monk, 1861

1. A-bide with me: fast falls the e-ven-tide;
The dark-ness deep-ens; Lord, with me a-bide!
When oth-er help-ers fail and com-forts flee,
Help of the help-less, O a-bide with me.

Abide with Me

1. Abide with me: fast falls the eventide;
   The darkness deepens; Lord, with me abide!
   When other helpers fail and comforts flee,
   Help of the helpless, O abide with me.

2. Swift to its close ebbs out life's little day;
   Earth's joys grow dim, its glories pass away;
   Change and decay in all around I see.
   O Thou who changest not, abide with me.

3. I need Thy presence every passing hour;
   What but Thy grace can foil the tempter's power?
   Who, like Thyself, my guide and stay can be?
   Through cloud and sunshine, Lord, abide with me.

4. Hold Thou Thy cross before my closing eyes;
   Shine through the gloom and point me to the skies:
   Heaven's morning breaks, and earth's vain shadows flee;
   In life, in death, O Lord, abide with me.

MORNING, EVENING, AND CLOSING

22 Now the Day Is Over

MERRIAL 6.5.6.5

Sabine Baring-Gould, 1865; alt.

Joseph Barnby, 1868

1. Now the day is o - ver,
Night is draw-ing nigh, Shad - ows of the eve - ning Steal a - cross the sky.

Now the Day Is Over

1. Now the day is over,
   Night is drawing nigh,
   Shadows of the evening
   Steal across the sky.

2. Jesus, give the weary
   Calm and sweet repose;
   With Thy tenderest blessing
   May mine eyelids close.

3. Comfort those who suffer,
   Watching late in pain;
   Those who plan some evil
   From their sin restrain.

4. When the morning wakens,
   Then may I arise
   Pure, and fresh, and sinless
   In Thy holy eyes.

MORNING, EVENING, AND CLOSING

23 Savior, Again to Thy Dear Name We Raise

ELLERS 10.10.10.10

John Ellerton, 1866   Edward John Hopkins, 1869

1. Savior, again to Thy dear name we raise
With one accord our parting hymn of praise.
We stand to bless Thee ere our worship cease;
And, now departing, wait Thy word of peace.

Savior, Again to Thy Dear Name We Raise

1. Savior, again to Thy dear name we raise
   With one accord our parting hymn of praise.
   We stand to bless Thee ere our worship cease;
   And, now departing, wait Thy word of peace.

2. Grant us Thy peace upon our homeward way;
   With Thee began, with Thee shall end the day.
   Guard Thou the lips from sin, the hearts from shame,
   That in this house have called upon Thy name.

3. Grant us Thy peace, Lord, through the coming night;
   Turn Thou for us its darkness into light.
   From harm and danger keep Thy children free,
   For dark and light are both alike to Thee.

4. Grant us Thy peace throughout our earthly life,
   Our balm in sorrow, and our stay in strife.
   Then, when Thy voice shall bid our conflict cease,
   Call us, O Lord, to Thine eternal peace.

MORNING, EVENING, AND CLOSING

24 Lord, Dismiss Us with Thy Blessing
SICILIAN MARINERS   8.7.8.7.8.7

Attr. John Fawcett, 1773
Stanza 1, line 6, alt. 1774, Conyer's *Collection of Psalms*
Stanza 3 alt. Godfrey Thring

Sicilian melody

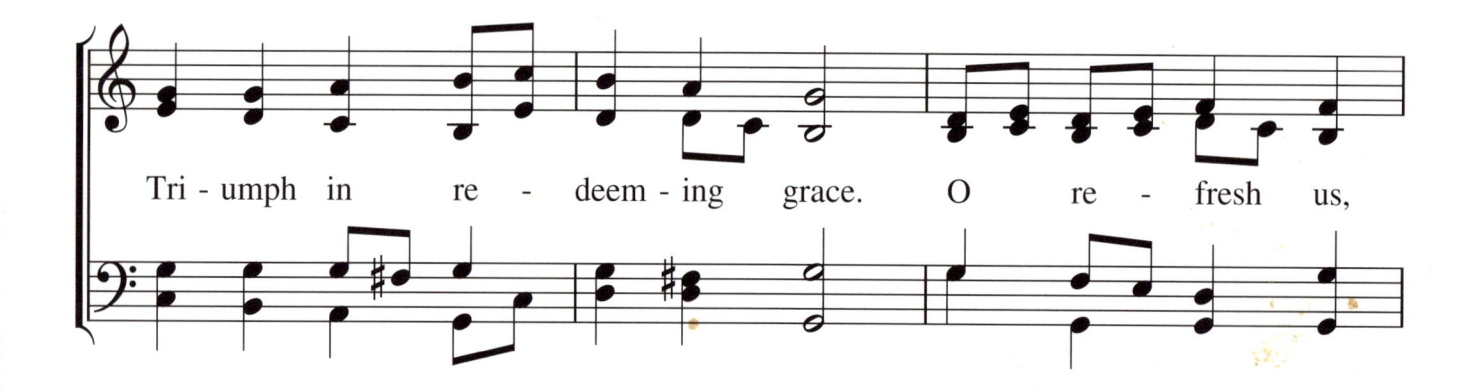

1. Lord, dismiss us with Thy blessing; Fill our hearts with joy and peace; Let us each, Thy love possessing, Triumph in redeeming grace. O refresh us, O refresh us, Trav'eling through this wilderness.

Lord, Dismiss Us with Thy Blessing

1. Lord, dismiss us with Thy blessing;
   Fill our hearts with joy and peace;
   Let us each, Thy love possessing,
   Triumph in redeeming grace.
   O refresh us, O refresh us,
   Traveling through this wilderness.

2. Thanks we give and adoration
   For Thy gospel's joyful sound;
   May the fruits of Thy salvation
   In our hearts and lives abound.
   Ever faithful, ever faithful
   To the truth may we be found:

3. So that when Thy love shall call us,
   Savior, from the world away,
   Let no fear of death appall us,
   Glad Thy summons to obey.
   May we ever, may we ever
   Reign with Thee in endless day.

LORD'S SUPPER

25 Here, O My Lord, I See Thee Face to Face

MORECAMBE 10.10.10.10

Horatius Bonar, 1855 — Frederick C. Atkinson, 1870

1. Here, O my Lord, I see Thee face to face;
Here would I touch and handle things unseen,
Here grasp with firmer hand eternal grace,
And all my weariness upon Thee lean.

Here, O My Lord, I See Thee Face to Face

1. Here, O my Lord, I see Thee face to face;
   Here would I touch and handle things unseen,
   Here grasp with firmer hand eternal grace,
   And all my weariness upon Thee lean.

2. Here would I feed upon the bread of God,
   Here drink with Thee the royal wine of heaven;
   Here would I lay aside each earthly load,
   Here taste afresh the calm of sin forgiven.

3. This is the hour of banquet and of song;
   This is the heavenly table spread for me;
   Here let me feast and, feasting, still prolong
   The brief, bright hour of fellowship with Thee.

4. I have no help but Thine, nor do I need
   Another arm save Thine to lean upon:
   It is enough, my Lord, enough indeed;
   My strength is in Thy might, Thy might alone.

LORD'S SUPPER

26 Jesus, Thou Joy of Loving Hearts

QUEBEC LM

Attr. Bernard of Clairvaux, c. 1150
Trans. Ray Palmer, 1858

Henry Baker, 1854

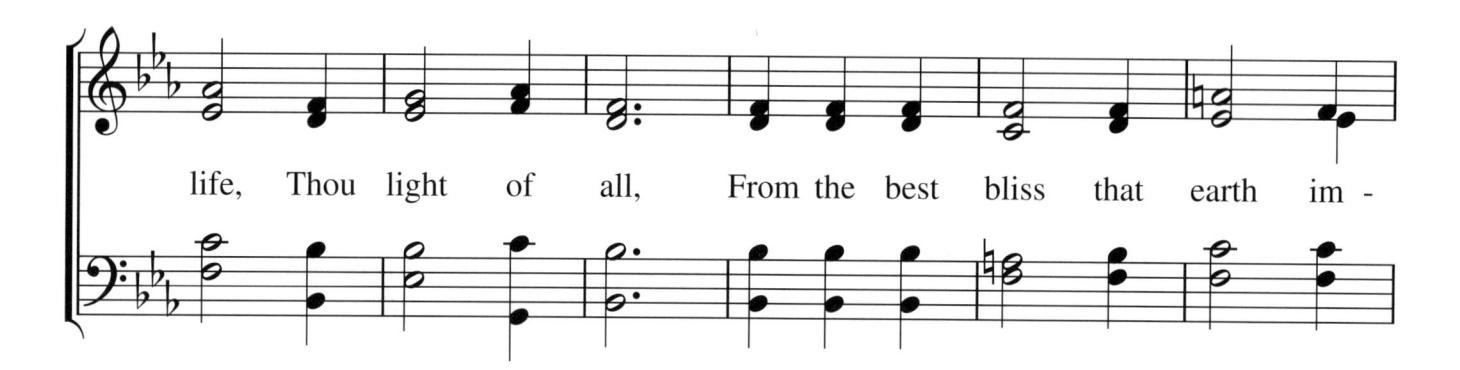

1. Jesus, Thou joy of loving hearts, Thou fount of life, Thou light of all, From the best bliss that earth imparts, We turn, unfilled, to heed Thy call.

Jesus, Thou Joy of Loving Hearts

1. Jesus, Thou joy of loving hearts,
   Thou fount of life, Thou light of all,
   From the best bliss that earth imparts,
   We turn, unfilled, to heed Thy call.

2. Thy truth unchanged hath ever stood;
   Thou savest those that on Thee call;
   To them that seek Thee Thou art good,
   To them that find Thee, all in all.

3. We taste Thee, O Thou living bread,
   And long to feast upon Thee still;
   We drink of Thee, the fountainhead,
   And thirst our souls from Thee to fill.

4. Our restless spirits yearn for Thee,
   Where'er our changeful lot is cast,
   Glad when Thy gracious smile we see,
   Blest when our faith can hold Thee fast.

5. O Jesus, ever with us stay,
   Make all our moments calm and bright;
   O chase the night of sin away,
   Shed o'er the world Thy holy light.

LORD'S SUPPER

27 Be Known to Us in Breaking Bread

ST. FLAVIAN   CM

James Montgomery, 1825 — From Day's *Psalter,* 1562

1. Be known to us in breaking bread, But do not then depart; Savior, abide with us, and spread Thy table in our heart.

Be Known to Us in Breaking Bread

1. Be known to us in breaking bread,
   But do not then depart;
   Savior, abide with us, and spread
   Thy table in our heart.

2. There sup with us in love divine;
   Thy body and Thy blood,
   That living bread, that heavenly wine,
   Be our immortal food.

LORD'S SUPPER

28 Let Us Break Bread Together

LET US BREAK BREAD   10.10 with refrain

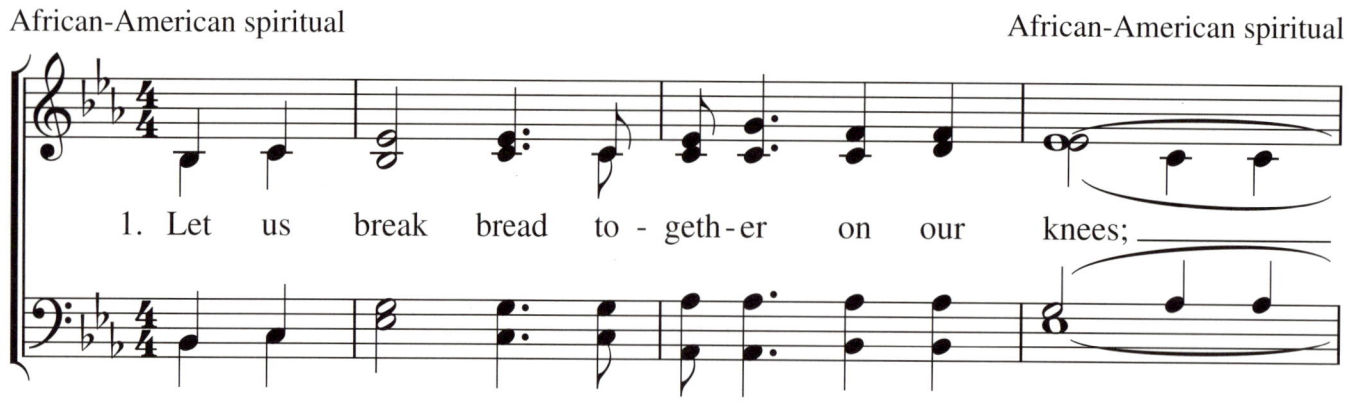

African-American spiritual											African-American spiritual

1. Let us break bread together on our knees; _____
Let us break bread together on our knees. _____

Refrain
When I fall on my knees, With my face to the rising sun, O Lord, have mercy on me. _____

Let Us Break Bread Together

1. Let us break bread together on our knees;
   Let us break bread together on our knees.
   > When I fall on my knees,
   > With my face to the rising sun,
   > O Lord, have mercy on me.

2. Let us drink wine together on our knees;
   Let us drink wine together on our knees.
   > When I fall on my knees,
   > With my face to the rising sun,
   > O Lord, have mercy on me.

3. Let us praise God together on our knees;
   Let us praise God together on our knees.
   > When I fall on my knees,
   > With my face to the rising sun,
   > O Lord, have mercy on me.

LORD'S SUPPER

29 Bread of the World in Mercy Broken

EUCHARISTIC HYMN 9.8.9.8 D

Reginald Heber, 1827 — John S. B. Hodges, 1868

1. Bread of the world in mer - cy bro - ken,
Wine of the soul in mer - cy shed,
By whom the words of life were spo - ken,
And in whose death our sins are dead.

Bread of the World in Mercy Broken

1. Bread of the world in mercy broken,
   Wine of the soul in mercy shed,
   By whom the words of life were spoken,
   And in whose death our sins are dead:

2. Look on the heart by sorrow broken,
   Look on the tears by sinners shed;
   And be Thy feast to us the token
   That by Thy grace our souls are fed.

ADVENT, CHRISTMAS, AND EPIPHANY

30 O Come, O Come, Emmanuel

VENI EMMANUEL   LM with refrain

Latin, c. 12th century
Stanzas 1–2 trans. John Mason Neale, 1851; alt. 1854
Stanza 3 trans. Henry Sloane Coffin, 1916

Plainsong, 13th century

1. O come, O come, Emmanuel, And ransom captive Israel, That mourns in lonely exile here, Until the Son of God appear. *Refrain* Rejoice! Rejoice! Emmanuel Shall come to thee, O Israel!

O Come, O Come, Emmanuel

1. O come, O come, Emmanuel,
   And ransom captive Israel,
   That mourns in lonely exile here,
   Until the Son of God appear.
   > Rejoice! Rejoice! Emmanuel
   > Shall come to thee, O Israel!

2. O come, Thou Dayspring, come and cheer
   Our spirits by Thine advent here;
   Disperse the gloomy clouds of night,
   And death's dark shadows put to flight.
   > Rejoice! Rejoice! Emmanuel
   > Shall come to thee, O Israel!

3. O come, Desire of nations, bind
   All peoples in one heart and mind;
   Bid envy, strife, and discord cease;
   Fill the whole world with heaven's peace.
   > Rejoice! Rejoice! Emmanuel
   > Shall come to thee, O Israel!

ADVENT, CHRISTMAS, AND EPIPHANY

31 Come, Thou Long-Expected Jesus

HYFRYDOL 8.7.8.7 D

Charles Wesley, 1744 — Rowland Hugh Prichard, 1831

1. Come, Thou long-expected Jesus, Born to set Thy people free; From our fears and sins release us; Let us find our rest in Thee. Israel's strength and consolation, Hope of all the earth Thou art; Dear desire of every nation, Joy of every longing heart.

Come, Thou Long-Expected Jesus

1. Come, Thou long-expected Jesus,
   Born to set Thy people free;
   From our fears and sins release us;
   Let us find our rest in Thee.
   Israel's strength and consolation,
   Hope of all the earth Thou art;
   Dear desire of every nation,
   Joy of every longing heart.

2. Born Thy people to deliver,
   Born a child and yet a King,
   Born to reign in us forever,
   Now Thy gracious kingdom bring.
   By Thine own eternal Spirit
   Rule in all our hearts alone;
   By Thine all-sufficient merit
   Raise us to Thy glorious throne.

ADVENT, CHRISTMAS, AND EPIPHANY

32 Lift Up Your Heads, Ye Mighty Gates
TRURO LM

Georg Weissel, 1642
Trans. Catherine Winkworth, 1855

Thomas Williams, 1789
Harm. Lowell Mason (1792–1872)

1. Lift up your heads, ye might-y gates, Be-hold the King of glo-ry waits; The King of kings is draw-ing near; The Sav-ior of the world is here!

Lift Up Your Heads, Ye Mighty Gates   32

1. Lift up your heads, ye mighty gates,
   Behold the King of glory waits;
   The King of kings is drawing near;
   The Savior of the world is here!

2. Fling wide the portals of your heart;
   Make it a temple, set apart
   From earthly use for heaven's employ,
   Adorned with prayer, and love, and joy.

3. Redeemer, come! I open wide
   My heart to Thee; here, Lord, abide.
   Let me Thy inner presence feel;
   Thy grace and love in me reveal.

ADVENT, CHRISTMAS, AND EPIPHANY

33 Watchman, Tell Us of the Night

ST. GEORGE'S WINDSOR 7.7.7.7 D

John Bowring, 1825; alt. 1972 George J. Elvey, 1859

1. Watch-man, tell us of the night, What its signs of prom-ise are.
Trav-eler, o'er yon moun-tain's height, See that glo-ry - beam-ing star.
Watch-man, doth its beau-teous ray Aught of joy or hope fore - tell?
Trav-eler, yes; it brings the day, Prom-ised day of Is - ra - el.

ADVENT, CHRISTMAS, AND EPIPHANY

Watchman, Tell Us of the Night   33

1. Watchman, tell us of the night,
   What its signs of promise are.
   Traveler, o'er yon mountain's height,
   See that glory-beaming star.
   Watchman, doth its beauteous ray
   Aught of joy or hope foretell?
   Traveler, yes; it brings the day,
   Promised day of Israel.

2. Watchman, tell us of the night,
   Higher yet that star ascends.
   Traveler, blessedness and light,
   Peace and truth its course portends.
   Watchman, will its beams alone
   Gild the spot that gave them birth?
   Traveler, ages are its own;
   See, it bursts o'er all the earth.

3. Watchman, tell us of the night,
   For the morning seems to dawn.
   Traveler, darkness takes its flight,
   Doubt and terror are withdrawn.
   Watchman, let your wanderings cease;
   Hasten to your quiet home.
   Traveler, lo, the Prince of Peace,
   Lo, the Son of God is come!

ADVENT, CHRISTMAS, AND EPIPHANY

34 O Come, All Ye Faithful

ADESTE FIDELES   6.6.10.5.6 with refrain

John Francis Wade (c. 1740–1743)
Trans. Frederick Oakeley, 1841

John Francis Wade (c. 1740–1743)
Harm. *The English Hymnal*, 1906

1. O come, all ye faithful, Joyful and triumphant, O come ye, O come ye to Bethlehem! Come and behold Him, Born the King of angels!

Refrain

O come, let us adore Him, O come, let us adore Him, O come let us adore Him, Christ, the Lord!

O Come, All Ye Faithful

34

1. O come, all ye faithful,
   Joyful and triumphant,
   O come ye, O come ye to Bethlehem!
   Come and behold Him,
   Born the King of angels!
       O come, let us adore Him,
       O come, let us adore Him,
       O come let us adore Him,
       Christ, the Lord!

2. Yea, Lord, we greet Thee,
   Born this happy morning,
   Jesus, to Thee be all glory given;
   Word of the Father,
   Now in flesh appearing!
       O come, let us adore Him,
       O come, let us adore Him,
       O come, let us adore Him,
       Christ, the Lord!

3. Sing, choirs of angels,
   Sing in exultation!
   Sing, all ye citizens of heaven above!
   Glory to God, all
   Glory in the highest!
       O come, let us adore Him,
       O come, let us adore Him,
       O come, let us adore Him,
       Christ, the Lord!

ADVENT, CHRISTMAS, AND EPIPHANY

35 O Little Town of Bethlehem
ST. LOUIS   8.6.8.6.7.6.8.6

Phillips Brooks, 1868

Lewis Henry Redner, 1868

1. O little town of Bethlehem, How still we see thee lie! Above thy deep and dreamless sleep The silent stars go by. Yet in thy dark streets shineth The everlasting light; The hopes and fears of all the years Are met in thee tonight.

O Little Town of Bethlehem

1. O little town of Bethlehem,
   How still we see thee lie!
   Above thy deep and dreamless sleep
   The silent stars go by.
   Yet in thy dark streets shineth
   The everlasting light;
   The hopes and fears of all the years
   Are met in thee tonight.

2. For Christ is born of Mary;
   And gathered all above,
   While mortals sleep, the angels keep
   Their watch of wondering love.
   O morning stars, together
   Proclaim the holy birth!
   And praises sing to God the King,
   And peace to all on earth.

3. O holy Child of Bethlehem,
   Descend to us, we pray;
   Cast out our sin and enter in,
   Be born in us today.
   We hear the Christmas angels
   The great glad tidings tell;
   O come to us, abide with us,
   Our Lord Emmanuel!

ADVENT, CHRISTMAS, AND EPIPHANY

36 Silent Night, Holy Night

STILLE NACHT   Irregular

Joseph Mohr, 1818
Trans. John Freeman Young, 1863

Franz Xavier Gruber, 1818

1. Silent night, holy night! All is calm, all is bright, Round yon virgin mother and child! Holy Infant so tender and mild, Sleep in heavenly peace, Sleep in heavenly peace.

ADVENT, CHRISTMAS, AND EPIPHANY

Silent Night, Holy Night 36

1. Silent night, holy night!
   All is calm, all is bright,
   Round yon virgin mother and child!
   Holy Infant so tender and mild,
   Sleep in heavenly peace,
   Sleep in heavenly peace.

2. Silent night, holy night!
   Shepherds quake at the sight,
   Glories stream from heaven afar,
   Heavenly hosts sing, "Alleluia;
   Christ the Savior is born,
   Christ the Savior is born."

3. Silent night, holy night!
   Son of God, love's pure light
   Radiant beams from Thy holy face,
   With the dawn of redeeming grace,
   Jesus, Lord, at Thy birth,
   Jesus, Lord, at Thy birth.

4. Silent night, holy night!
   Wondrous star, lend thy light;
   With the angels let us sing,
   Alleluia to our King;
   Christ the Savior is born,
   Christ the Savior is born.

ADVENT, CHRISTMAS, AND EPIPHANY

37 What Child Is This

GREENSLEEVES 8.7.8.7 with refrain

William Chatterton Dix, 1871

English ballad, 16th century
Arr. *Christmas Carols New and Old,* 1871

1. What Child is this, who, laid to rest, On Mary's lap is sleeping? Whom angels greet with anthems sweet While shepherds watch are keeping?

Refrain

This, this is Christ the King, whom shepherds guard and angels sing; Haste, haste to bring Him laud, the Babe, the Son of Mary!

What Child Is This

1. What Child is this, who, laid to rest,
   On Mary's lap is sleeping?
   Whom angels greet with anthems sweet
   While shepherds watch are keeping?
      This, this is Christ the King,
      Whom shepherds guard and angels sing;
      Haste, haste to bring Him laud,
      The Babe, the Son of Mary!

2. Why lies He in such mean estate
   Where ox and ass are feeding?
   Good Christian, fear; for sinners here
   The silent Word is pleading.
      This, this is Christ the King,
      Whom shepherds guard and angels sing;
      Haste, haste to bring Him laud,
      The Babe, the Son of Mary!

3. So bring Him incense, gold, and myrrh;
   Come, one and all, to own Him.
   The King of kings salvation brings;
   Let loving hearts enthrone Him.
      This, this is Christ the King,
      Whom shepherds guard and angels sing;
      Haste, haste to bring Him laud,
      The Babe, the Son of Mary!

ADVENT, CHRISTMAS, AND EPIPHANY

38 Away in a Manger

MUELLER 11.11.11.11

Stanzas 1–2, *Little Children's Book for Schools and Families,* c. 1885
Stanza 3, Gabriel's *Vineyard Songs,* 1892

Attr. James R. Murray, 1887

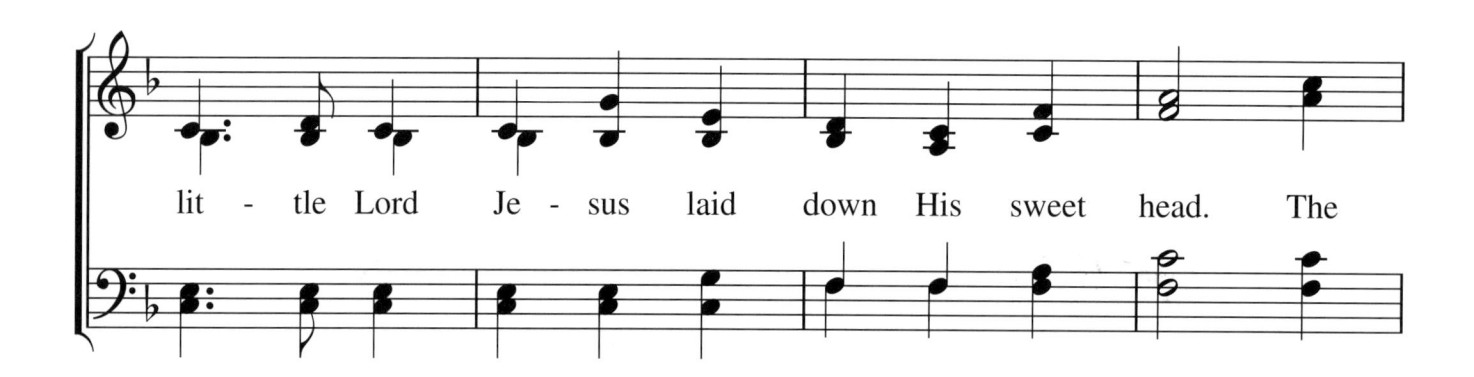

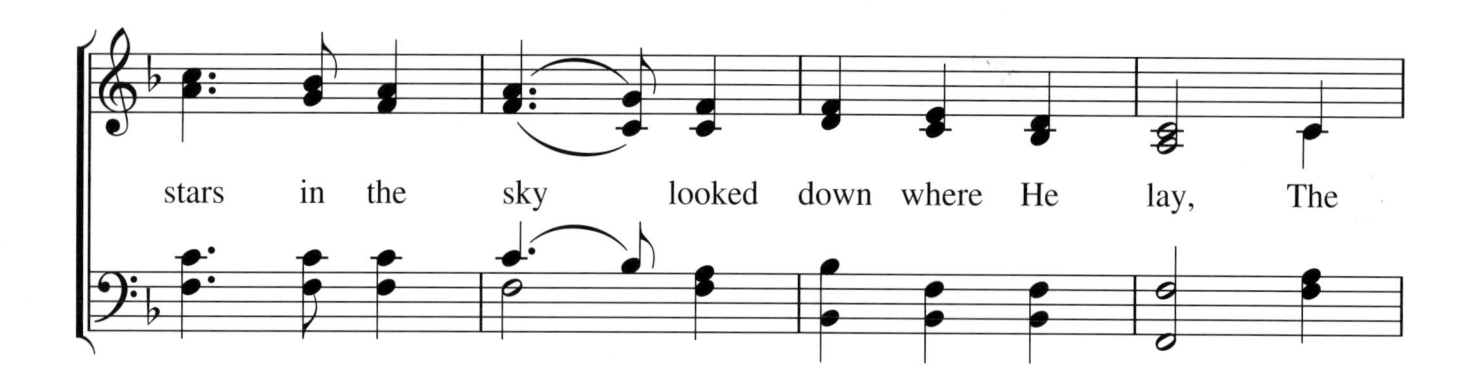

1. A-way in a man-ger, no crib for His bed, The lit-tle Lord Je-sus laid down His sweet head. The stars in the sky looked down where He lay, The lit-tle Lord Je-sus, a-sleep on the hay.

Away in a Manger   38

1. Away in a manger, no crib for His bed,
   The little Lord Jesus laid down His sweet head.
   The stars in the sky looked down where He lay,
   The little Lord Jesus, asleep on the hay.

2. The cattle are lowing, the poor Baby wakes,
   But little Lord Jesus, no crying he makes.
   I love Thee, Lord Jesus, look down from the sky,
   And stay by my side until morning is nigh.

3. Be near me, Lord Jesus; I ask Thee to stay
   Close by me forever and love me, I pray.
   Bless all the dear children in Thy tender care,
   And fit us for heaven to live with Thee there.

ADVENT, CHRISTMAS, AND EPIPHANY

39 Hark! The Herald Angels Sing

MENDELSSOHN 7.7.7.7 D with refrain

Charles Wesley, 1739; alt.

Felix Mendelssohn, 1840
Arr. William Hayman Cummings, 1855

1. Hark! The herald angels sing, "Glory to the new-born King.
Peace on earth, and mercy mild, God and sinners reconciled!"
Joyful, all ye nations, rise, Join the triumph of the skies;
With the angelic host proclaim, "Christ is born in Bethlehem!"
Hark! The herald angels sing, "Glory to the new-born King!"

Hark! The Herald Angels Sing

1. Hark! The herald angels sing,
   "Glory to the newborn King.
   Peace on earth, and mercy mild,
   God and sinners reconciled!"
   Joyful, all ye nations, rise,
   Join the triumph of the skies;
   With the angelic host proclaim,
   "Christ is born in Bethlehem!"
   Hark! The herald angels sing,
   "Glory to the newborn King!"

2. Hail the heaven-born Prince of Peace!
   Hail the sun of righteousness!
   Light and life to all He brings,
   Risen with healing in His wings.
   Mild He lays His glory by,
   Born that we no more may die,
   Born to raise us from the earth,
   Born to give us second birth.
   Hark! The herald angels sing,
   "Glory to the newborn King!"

ADVENT, CHRISTMAS, AND EPIPHANY

40 It Came Upon the Midnight Clear

CAROL CMD

Edmund Hamilton Sears, 1849

Richard Storrs Willis, 1850

1. It came up-on the mid-night clear, That glo-rious song of old, From an-gels bend-ing near the earth, To touch their harps of gold: "Peace on the earth, good will to all, From heaven's all-gra-cious King": The world in sol-emn still-ness lay, To hear the an-gels sing.

It Came Upon the Midnight Clear

1. It came upon the midnight clear,
   That glorious song of old,
   From angels bending near the earth,
   To touch their harps of gold:
   "Peace on the earth, good will to all,
   From heaven's all-gracious King":
   The world in solemn stillness lay,
   To hear the angels sing.

2. Still through the cloven skies they come,
   With peaceful wings unfurled,
   And still their heavenly music floats
   O'er all the weary world:
   Above its sad and lowly plains
   They bend on hovering wing,
   And ever o'er its Babel sounds
   The blessed angels sing.

3. For lo, the days are hastening on,
   By prophet bards foretold,
   When with the ever-circling years
   Comes round the age of gold;
   When peace shall over all the earth
   Its ancient splendors fling,
   And the whole world give back the song
   Which now the angels sing.

ADVENT, CHRISTMAS, AND EPIPHANY

41 The First Nowell

THE FIRST NOWELL   Irregular with refrain

English carol, 17th century

English carol
Sandys' *Christmas Carols,* 1833

1. The first Nowell the angel did say Was to certain poor shepherds in fields as they lay; In fields where they lay keeping their sheep, On a cold winter's night that was so deep.

Refrain
Nowell, Nowell, Nowell, Nowell, Born is the King of Israel.

The First Nowell

1. The first Nowell the angel did say
   Was to certain poor shepherds in fields as they lay;
   In fields where they lay keeping their sheep,
   On a cold winter's night that was so deep.
   Nowell, Nowell, Nowell, Nowell,
   Born is the King of Israel.

2. They lookèd up and saw a star
   Shining in the east beyond them far,
   And to the earth it gave great light,
   And so it continued both day and night.
   Nowell, Nowell, Nowell, Nowell,
   Born is the King of Israel.

3. This star drew nigh to the northwest;
   O'er Bethlehem it took its rest;
   And there it did both stop and stay,
   Right over the place where Jesus lay.
   Nowell, Nowell, Nowell, Nowell,
   Born is the King of Israel.

ADVENT, CHRISTMAS, AND EPIPHANY

42 While Shepherds Watched Their Flocks

CHRISTMAS   CM with repeat

Nahum Tate, 1700; alt. 1987

George Frederick Handel, 1728
Arr. Lowell Mason, 1821

1. While shepherds watched their flocks by night, All seated on the ground, The angel of the Lord came down, And glory shone around, And glory shone around.

While Shepherds Watched Their Flocks

1. While shepherds watched their flocks by night,
   All seated on the ground,
   The angel of the Lord came down,
   And glory shone around,
   And glory shone around.

2. "Fear not," said he, for mighty dread
   Had seized their troubled mind;
   "Glad tidings of great joy I bring
   To you and humankind,
   To you and humankind.

3. "To you, in David's town this day,
   Is born of David's line
   The Savior, who is Christ the Lord,
   And this shall be the sign,
   And this shall be the sign.

4. "The heavenly Babe you there shall find
   To human view displayed,
   And humbly wrapped in swathing bands,
   And in a manger laid,
   And in a manger laid."

ADVENT, CHRISTMAS, AND EPIPHANY

43 Joy to the World!

ANTIOCH   CM with repeat

Isaac Watts, 1719; alt.

Attr. George Frederick Handel, 1741
Arr. Lowell Mason, 1836

1. Joy to the world! the Lord is come: Let earth receive her King; Let every heart prepare Him room, And heaven and nature sing, And heaven and nature sing, And heaven, and heaven and nature sing.

Joy to the World!

1. Joy to the world! the Lord is come:
   Let earth receive her King;
   Let every heart prepare Him room,
   And heaven and nature sing,
   And heaven and nature sing,
   And heaven, and heaven and nature sing.

2. Joy to the world! the Savior reigns:
   Let us our songs employ;
   While fields and floods, rocks, hills, and plains
   Repeat the sounding joy,
   Repeat the sounding joy,
   Repeat, repeat the sounding joy.

3. No more let sins and sorrows grow,
   Nor thorns infest the ground;
   He comes to make His blessings flow
   Far as the curse is found,
   Far as the curse is found,
   Far as, far as the curse is found.

4. He rules the world with truth and grace,
   And makes the nations prove
   The glories of His righteousness,
   And wonders of His love,
   And wonders of His love,
   And wonders, wonders of His love.

ADVENT, CHRISTMAS, AND EPIPHANY

44 As with Gladness Men of Old

DIX 7.7.7.7.7.7

William Chatterton Dix, c. 1858

Conrad Kocher, 1838
Abr. William Henry Monk, 1861
Harm. *The English Hymnal,* 1906

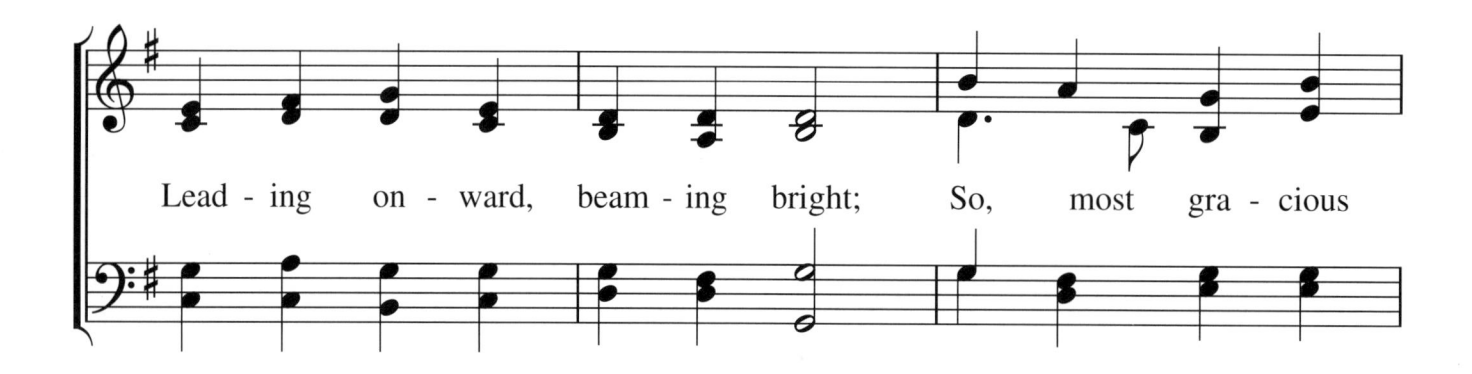

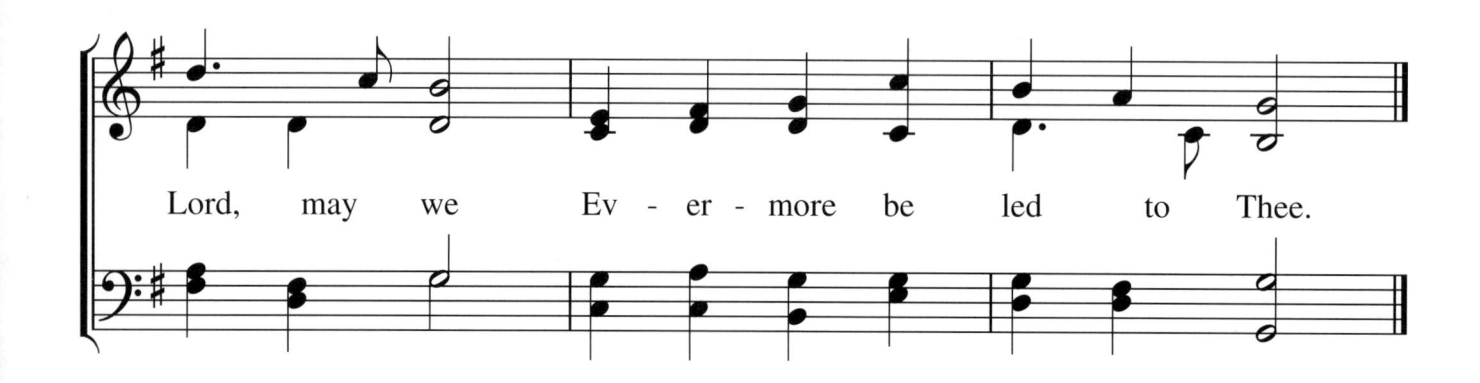

1. As with gladness men of old Did the guiding star behold; As with joy they hailed its light, Leading onward, beaming bright; So, most gracious Lord, may we Evermore be led to Thee.

As with Gladness Men of Old

1. As with gladness men of old
   Did the guiding star behold;
   As with joy they hailed its light,
   Leading onward, beaming bright;
   So, most gracious Lord, may we
   Evermore be led to Thee.

2. As with joyful steps they sped
   To that lowly manger bed,
   There to bend the knee before
   Him whom heaven and earth adore;
   So may we with willing feet
   Ever seek Thy mercy seat.

3. Holy Jesus, every day
   Keep us in the narrow way;
   And, when earthly things are past,
   Bring our ransomed souls at last
   Where they need no star to guide,
   Where no clouds Thy glory hide.

ADVENT, CHRISTMAS, AND EPIPHANY

45 We Three Kings of Orient Are

THREE KINGS OF ORIENT   8.8.4.4.6 with refrain

John H. Hopkins, Jr., 1857   John H. Hopkins, Jr., 1857

1. We three kings of O - ri - ent are; Bear-ing gifts we trav-erse a - far,

Field and foun - tain, moor and moun - tain, Fol-low-ing yon - der star.

Refrain

O star of won - der, star of night, Star with roy - al beau - ty bright,

West-ward lead - ing, still pro - ceed - ing, Guide us to thy per - fect light!

ADVENT, CHRISTMAS, AND EPIPHANY

We Three Kings of Orient Are

45

1. We three kings of Orient are;
   Bearing gifts we traverse afar,
   Field and fountain, moor and mountain,
   Following yonder star.
   > O star of wonder, star of night,
   > Star with royal beauty bright,
   > Westward leading, still proceeding,
   > Guide us to thy perfect light!

(Stanzas 2, 3, and 4 may be read or sung as solos.)

5. Glorious now behold Him arise,
   King and God and Sacrifice;
   Alleluia, Alleluia
   Sounds through the earth and skies.
   > O star of wonder, star of night,
   > Star with royal beauty bright,
   > Westward leading, still proceeding,
   > Guide us to thy perfect light!

HOLY WEEK AND EASTER

46 All Glory, Laud, and Honor

VALET WILL ICH DIR GEBEN 7.6.7.6 D

Theodulph of Orleans, c. 829
Trans. John Mason Neale, 1851; alt. 1859

Melchior Teschner, 1614
Arr. William Henry Monk, 1861

Refrain

1. All glory, laud, and honor To Thee, Redeemer, King! To whom the lips of children Made sweet hosannas ring. *fine*

Thou art the King of Israel, Thou David's royal Son, Who in the Lord's name comest, The King and blessed One. *Repeat Refrain*

All Glory, Laud, and Honor

HOLY WEEK AND EASTER 46

Refrain
All glory, laud, and honor
To Thee, Redeemer, King!
To whom the lips of children
Made sweet hosannas ring.

1. Thou art the King of Israel,
   Thou David's royal Son,
   Who in the Lord's name comest,
   The King and blessed One.

   Refrain

2. The people of the Hebrews
   With palms before Thee went;
   Our praise and prayers and anthems
   Before Thee we present.

   Refrain

3. Thou didst accept their praises;
   Accept the prayers we bring,
   Who in all good delightest,
   Thou good and gracious King!

   Refrain

HOLY WEEK AND EASTER

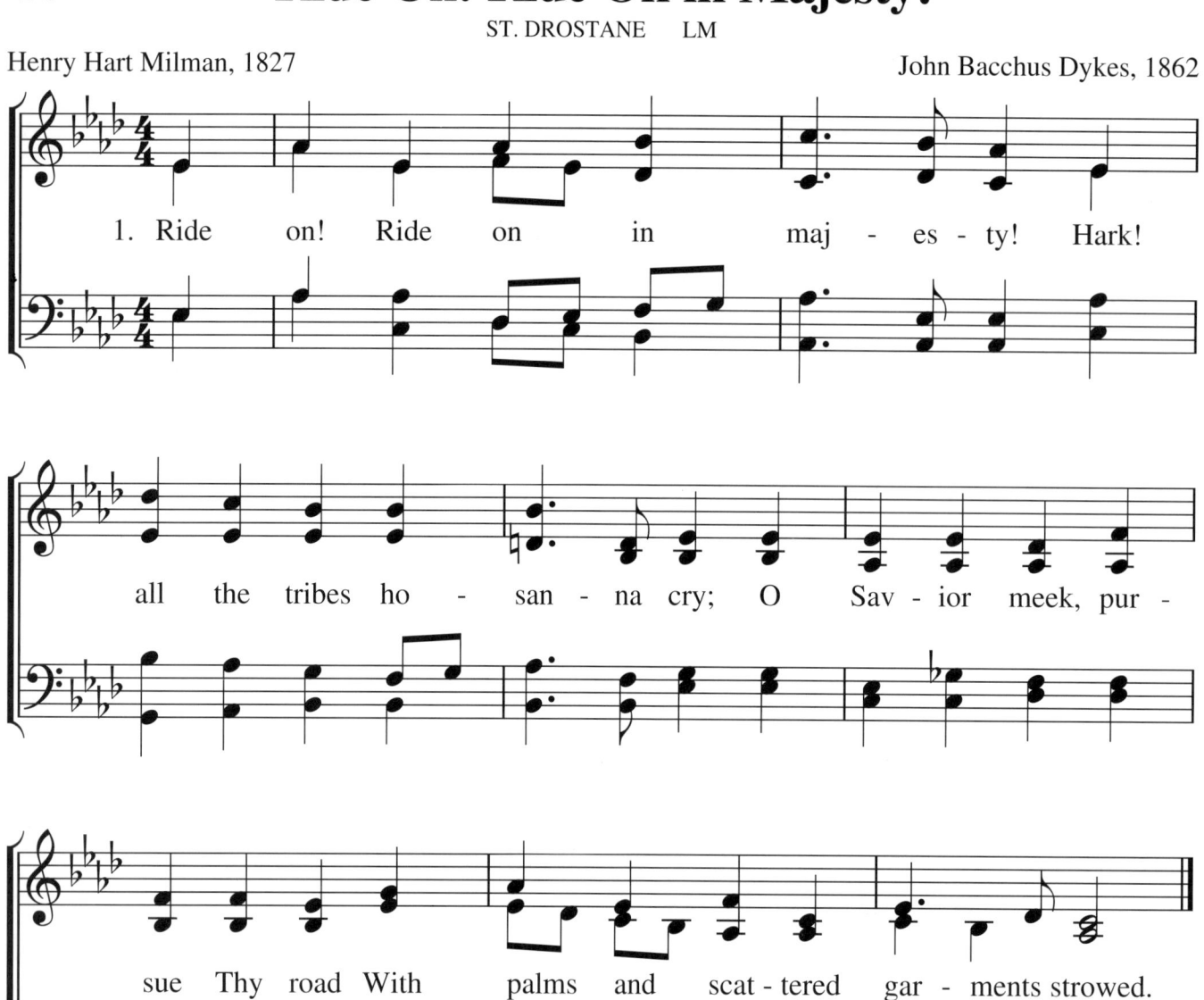

47 Ride On! Ride On in Majesty!

ST. DROSTANE LM

Henry Hart Milman, 1827

John Bacchus Dykes, 1862

1. Ride on! Ride on in majesty! Hark! all the tribes hosanna cry; O Savior meek, pursue Thy road With palms and scattered garments strowed.

Ride On! Ride On in Majesty!

1. Ride on! Ride on in majesty!
   Hark! all the tribes hosanna cry;
   O Savior meek, pursue Thy road
   With palms and scattered garments strowed.

2. Ride on! Ride on in majesty!
   In lowly pomp ride on to die:
   O Christ, Thy triumphs now begin
   O'er captive death and conquered sin.

3. Ride on! Ride on in majesty!
   The winged squadrons of the sky
   Look down with sad and wondering eyes
   To see the approaching sacrifice.

4. Ride on! Ride on in majesty!
   In lowly pomp ride on to die;
   Bow Thy meek head to mortal pain,
   Then take, O God, Thy power, and reign.

HOLY WEEK AND EASTER

48 O Sacred Head, Now Wounded

PASSION CHORALE 7.6.7.6 D

Attr. Bernard of Clairvaux (1091–1153)
Trans. James Waddell Alexander, 1830

Hans Leo Hassler, 1601
Harm. Johann Sebastian Bach, 1729

1. O sacred head, now wounded, With grief and shame weighed down; Now scornfully surrounded With thorns, Thine only crown; O sacred head, what glory, What bliss till now was Thine! Yet, though despised and gory, I joy to call Thee mine.

O Sacred Head, Now Wounded

1. O sacred head, now wounded,
   With grief and shame weighed down;
   Now scornfully surrounded
   With thorns, Thine only crown;
   O sacred head, what glory,
   What bliss till now was Thine!
   Yet, though despised and gory,
   I joy to call Thee mine.

2. What Thou, my Lord, hast suffered
   Was all for sinners' gain:
   Mine, mine was the transgression,
   But Thine the deadly pain.
   Lo, here I fall, my Savior!
   'Tis I deserve Thy place;
   Look on me with Thy favor,
   Vouchsafe to me Thy grace.

3. What language shall I borrow
   To thank Thee, dearest friend,
   For this Thy dying sorrow,
   Thy pity without end?
   O make me Thine forever;
   And should I fainting be,
   Lord, let me never, never
   Outlive my love to Thee.

HOLY WEEK AND EASTER

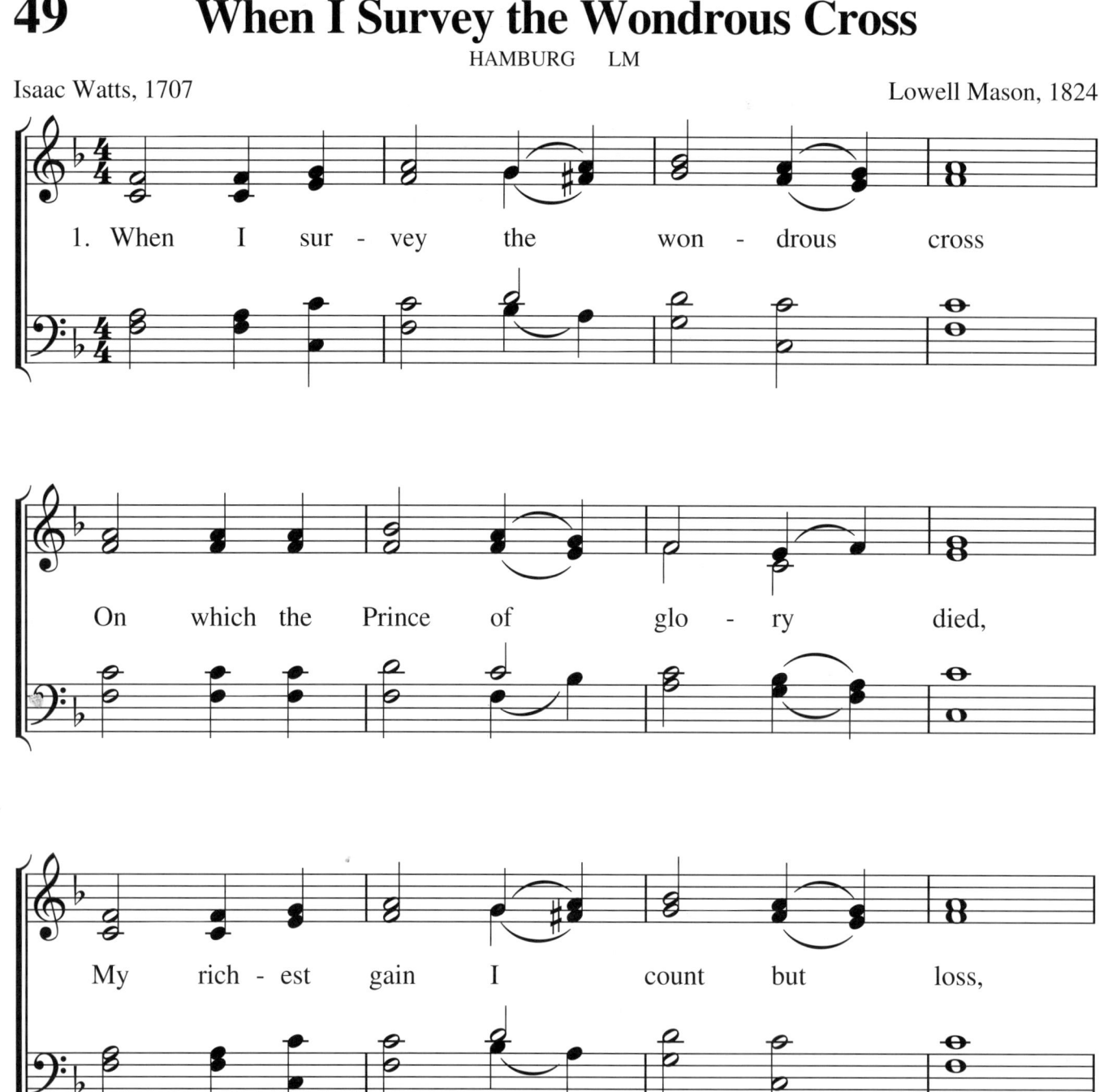

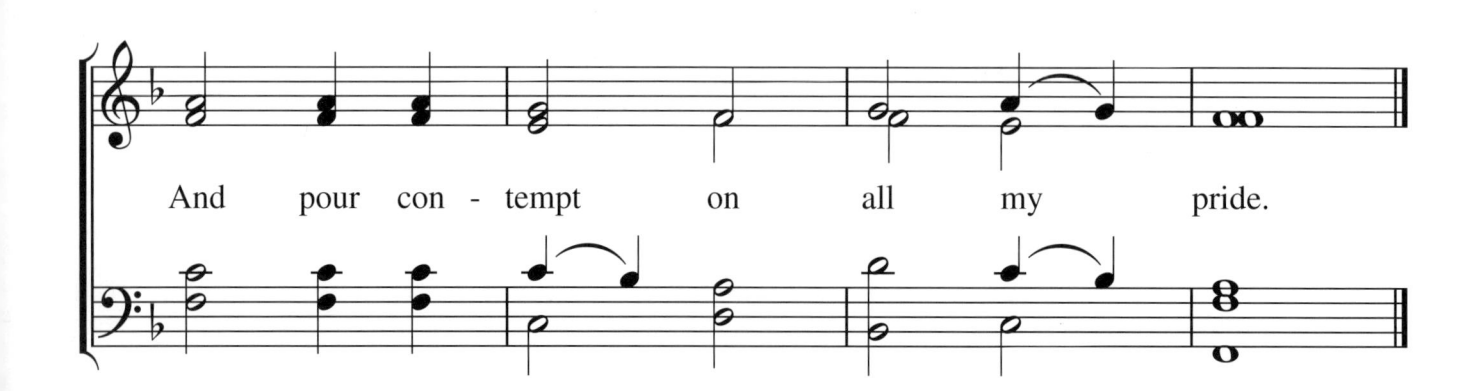

49 When I Survey the Wondrous Cross

HAMBURG LM

Isaac Watts, 1707   Lowell Mason, 1824

1. When I survey the wondrous cross
On which the Prince of glory died,
My richest gain I count but loss,
And pour contempt on all my pride.

When I Survey the Wondrous Cross

1. When I survey the wondrous cross
   On which the Prince of glory died,
   My richest gain I count but loss,
   And pour contempt on all my pride.

2. Forbid it, Lord, that I should boast,
   Save in the death of Christ my God;
   All the vain things that charm me most,
   I sacrifice them to His blood.

3. See, from His head, His hands, His feet,
   Sorrow and love flow mingled down;
   Did e'er such love and sorrow meet,
   Or thorns compose so rich a crown?

4. Were the whole realm of nature mine,
   That were a present far too small;
   Love so amazing, so divine,
   Demands my soul, my life, my all.

HOLY WEEK AND EASTER

50   In the Cross of Christ I Glory

RATHBUN   8.7.8.7

John Bowring, 1825   Ithamar Conkey, 1849

1. In the cross of Christ I glory,
Towering o'er the wrecks of time;
All the light of sacred story
Gathers round its head sublime.

In the Cross of Christ I Glory

1. In the cross of Christ I glory,
   Towering o'er the wrecks of time;
   All the light of sacred story
   Gathers round its head sublime.

2. When the woes of life o'ertake me,
   Hopes deceive, and fears annoy,
   Never shall the cross forsake me:
   Lo! it glows with peace and joy.

3. When the sun of bliss is beaming
   Light and love upon my way,
   From the cross the radiance streaming
   Adds more luster to the day.

4. Bane and blessing, pain and pleasure,
   By the cross are sanctified;
   Peace is there that knows no measure,
   Joys that through all time abide.

HOLY WEEK AND EASTER

51

Were You There?

WERE YOU THERE   Irregular

African-American spiritual   African-American spiritual

1. Were you there when they cru-ci-fied my Lord? _____ Were you there when they cru-ci-fied my Lord? Oh! _____ Some-times it caus-es me to trem-ble, trem-ble, trem-ble. _____ Were you there when they cru-ci-fied my Lord? _____

Were You There?

1. Were you there when they crucified my Lord?
   Were you there when they crucified my Lord?
   Oh! Sometimes it causes me to tremble,
   tremble, tremble.
   Were you there when they crucified my Lord?

2. Were you there when they nailed Him to the tree?
   Were you there when they nailed Him to the tree?
   Oh! Sometimes it causes me to tremble,
   tremble, tremble.
   Were you there when they nailed Him to the tree?

3. Were you there when they laid Him in the tomb?
   Were you there when they laid Him in the tomb?
   Oh! Sometimes it causes me to tremble,
   tremble, tremble.
   Were you there when they laid Him in the tomb?

HOLY WEEK AND EASTER

52 Beneath the Cross of Jesus
ST. CHRISTOPHER 7.6.8.6.8.6.8.6

Elizabeth Cecilia Douglas Clephane, 1868 — Frederick Charles Maker, 1881

1. Beneath the cross of Jesus I fain would take my stand, The shadow of a mighty rock Within a weary land; A home within the wilderness, A rest upon the way, From the burning of the noontide heat, And the burden of the day.

Beneath the Cross of Jesus

1. Beneath the cross of Jesus
   I fain would take my stand,
   The shadow of a mighty rock
   Within a weary land;
   A home within the wilderness,
   A rest upon the way,
   From the burning of the noontide heat,
   And the burden of the day.

2. Upon the cross of Jesus
   Mine eye at times can see
   The very dying form of One
   Who suffered there for me:
   And from my stricken heart with tears
   Two wonders I confess:
   The wonders of redeeming love
   And my unworthiness.

HOLY WEEK AND EASTER

53 Jesus Christ Is Risen Today

EASTER HYMN   7.7.7.7 with alleluias

Stanzas 1–3, *Lyra Davidica,* 1708
Stanza 4, Charles Wesley, 1740

Lyra Davidica, 1708
Adapted from *The Compleat Psalmodist,* 1749

1. Je-sus Christ is risen to-day, Al - le - lu - ia!
Our tri-umph-ant ho-ly day, Al - le - lu - ia!
Who did once up-on the cross, Al - le - lu - ia!
Suf-fer to re-deem our loss. Al - le - lu - ia!

Jesus Christ Is Risen Today

1. Jesus Christ is risen today, Alleluia!
   Our triumphant holy day, Alleluia!
   Who did once upon the cross, Alleluia!
   Suffer to redeem our loss. Alleluia!

2. Hymns of praise then let us sing, Alleluia!
   Unto Christ, our heavenly King, Alleluia!
   Who endured the cross and grave, Alleluia!
   Sinners to redeem and save. Alleluia!

3. But the pains which He endured, Alleluia!
   Our salvation have procured, Alleluia!
   Now above the sky He's King, Alleluia!
   Where the angels ever sing. Alleluia!

4. Sing we to our God above, Alleluia!
   Praise eternal as God's love, Alleluia!
   Praise our God, ye heavenly host, Alleluia!
   Father, Son, and Holy Ghost. Alleluia!

HOLY WEEK AND EASTER

54 Come, Ye Faithful, Raise the Strain
ST. KEVIN   7.6.7.6 D

John of Damascus (c. 675–749)
Trans. John Mason Neale, 1859; alt.

Arthur S. Sullivan (1842–1900); alt.

1. Come, ye faithful, raise the strain Of triumphant gladness;
God hath brought forth Israel Into joy from sadness;
Loosed from Pharaoh's bitter yoke Jacob's sons and daughters;
Led them, with unmoistened foot, Through the Red Sea waters.

HOLY WEEK AND EASTER

Come, Ye Faithful, Raise the Strain   54

1. Come, ye faithful, raise the strain
 Of triumphant gladness;
 God hath brought forth Israel
 Into joy from sadness;
 Loosed from Pharaoh's bitter yoke
 Jacob's sons and daughters;
 Led them, with unmoistened foot,
 Through the Red Sea waters.

2. 'Tis the spring of souls today;
 Christ hath burst His prison,
 And from three days' sleep in death
 As a sun hath risen.
 Now rejoice, Jerusalem,
 And with true affection
 Welcome in unwearied strains
 Jesus' resurrection!

HOLY WEEK AND EASTER

55 The Day of Resurrection!

LANCASHIRE 7.6.7.6 D

John of Damascus (c. 675–749)
Trans. John Mason Neale, 1862

Henry T. Smart, 1835

1. The day of res-ur-rec-tion! Earth, tell it out a-broad; The Pass-o-ver of glad-ness, The Pass-o-ver of God. From death to life e-ter-nal, From this world to the sky, Our Christ hath brought us o-ver With hymns of vic-to-ry.

HOLY WEEK AND EASTER

The Day of Resurrection! 55

1. The day of resurrection!
   Earth, tell it out abroad;
   The Passover of gladness,
   The Passover of God.
   From death to life eternal,
   From this world to the sky,
   Our Christ hath brought us over
   With hymns of victory.

2. Our hearts be pure from evil,
   That we may see aright
   The Lord in rays eternal
   Of resurrection light;
   And, listening to His accents,
   May hear, so calm and plain,
   His own "All hail!" and, hearing,
   May raise the victor strain.

3. Now let the heavens be joyful,
   Let earth the song begin,
   Let the round world keep triumph,
   And all that is therein;
   Let all things seen and unseen
   Their notes of gladness blend,
   For Christ the Lord is risen,
   Our joy that hath no end.

PENTECOST AND HOLY SPIRIT

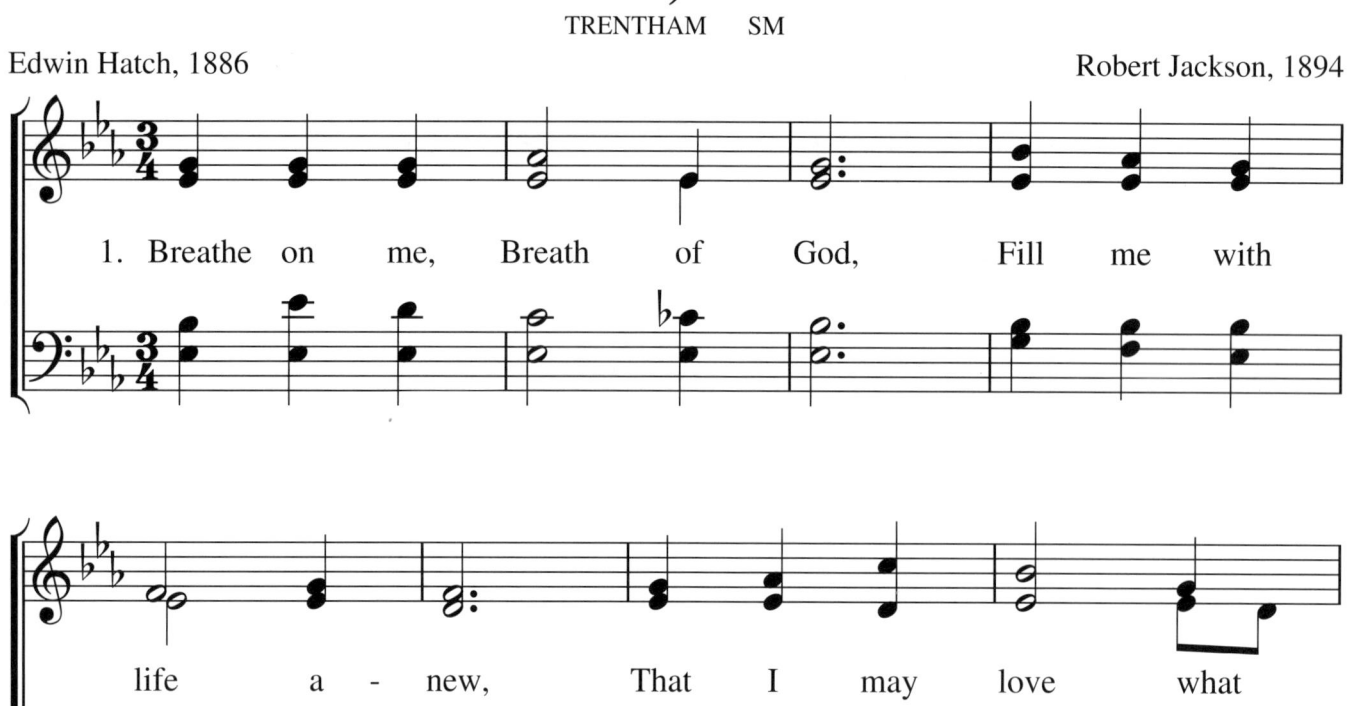

56 Breathe on Me, Breath of God
TRENTHAM SM

Edwin Hatch, 1886 — Robert Jackson, 1894

1. Breathe on me, Breath of God, Fill me with life anew, That I may love what Thou dost love, And do what Thou wouldst do.

Breathe on Me, Breath of God

56

PENTECOST AND HOLY SPIRIT

1. Breathe on me, Breath of God,
   Fill me with life anew,
   That I may love what Thou dost love,
   And do what Thou wouldst do.

2. Breathe on me, Breath of God,
   Until my heart is pure,
   Until with Thee I will one will,
   To do and to endure.

3. Breathe on me, Breath of God,
   Till I am wholly Thine,
   Till all this earthly part of me
   Glows with Thy fire divine.

4. Breathe on me, Breath of God,
   So shall I never die,
   But live with Thee the perfect life
   Of Thine eternity.

PENTECOST AND HOLY SPIRIT

57 Come, Holy Spirit, Heavenly Dove
ST. AGNES CM

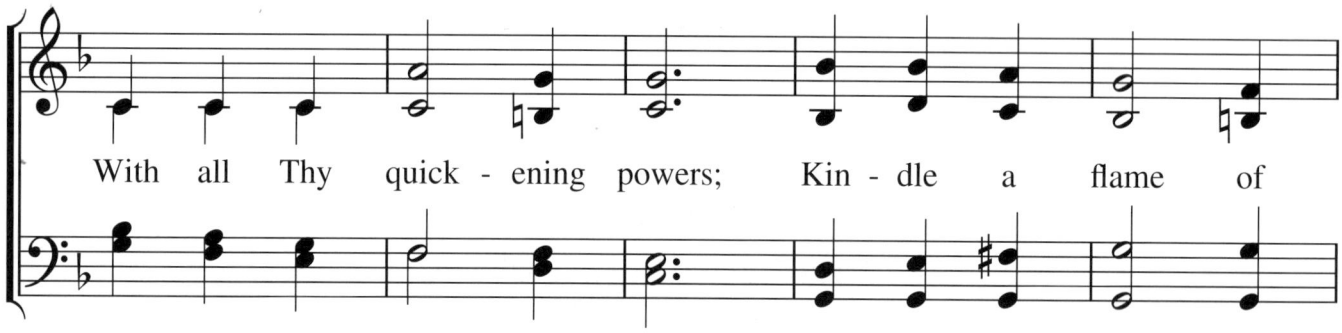

Isaac Watts, 1707 — John Bacchus Dykes, 1866

1. Come, Holy Spirit, heavenly Dove,
With all Thy quickening powers;
Kindle a flame of sacred love
In these cold hearts of ours.

Come, Holy Spirit, Heavenly Dove   57

1. Come, Holy Spirit, heavenly Dove,
   With all Thy quickening powers;
   Kindle a flame of sacred love
   In these cold hearts of ours.

2. In vain we tune our formal songs,
   In vain we strive to rise;
   Hosannas languish on our tongues,
   And our devotion dies.

3. Dear Lord, and shall we ever live
   At this poor dying rate?
   Our love so faint, so cold to Thee,
   And Thine to us so great!

4. Come, Holy Spirit, heavenly Dove,
   With all Thy quickening powers;
   Come, shed abroad a Savior's love,
   And that shall kindle ours.

PENTECOST AND HOLY SPIRIT

58 Holy Spirit, Truth Divine

MERCY 7.7.7.7

Samuel Longfellow, 1864

Arr. from Louis M. Gottschalk, 1867

1. Holy Spirit, truth divine,
Dawn upon this soul of mine;
Word of God, and inward light,
Wake my spirit, clear my sight.

Holy Spirit, Truth Divine

1. Holy Spirit, truth divine,
   Dawn upon this soul of mine;
   Word of God, and inward light,
   Wake my spirit, clear my sight.

2. Holy Spirit, love divine,
   Glow within this heart of mine;
   Kindle every high desire;
   Perish self in Thy pure fire.

3. Holy Spirit, power divine,
   Fill and nerve this will of mine;
   By Thee may I strongly live,
   Bravely bear, and nobly strive.

4. Holy Spirit, right divine,
   Make my conscience wholly Thine;
   Be my law, and I shall be
   Firmly bound, forever free.

PENTECOST AND HOLY SPIRIT

59 Spirit of God, Descend Upon My Heart

MORECAMBE   10.10.10.10

George Croly, 1854

Frederick Cook Atkinson, 1870

1. Spirit of God, descend upon my heart;
Wean it from earth, through all its pulses move;
Stoop to my weakness, mighty as Thou art,
And make me love Thee as I ought to love.

Spirit of God, Descend Upon My Heart   59

1. Spirit of God, descend upon my heart;
   Wean it from earth, through all its pulses move;
   Stoop to my weakness, mighty as Thou art,
   And make me love Thee as I ought to love.

2. Hast Thou not bid us love Thee, God and King;
   All, all Thine own: soul, heart, and strength, and mind?
   I see Thy cross, there teach my heart to cling.
   O let me seek Thee, and O let me find!

3. Teach me to feel that Thou art always nigh;
   Teach me the struggles of the soul to bear,
   To check the rising doubt, the rebel sigh;
   Teach me the patience of unanswered prayer.

4. Teach me to love Thee as Thine angels love,
   One holy passion filling all my frame;
   The baptism of the heaven-descended Dove,
   My heart an altar, and Thy love the flame.

DISCIPLESHIP

60

Jesus Calls Us

GALILEE 8.7.8.7

Cecil Frances Alexander, 1852

William H. Jude, 1887

1. Jesus calls us o'er the tumult Of our life's wild, restless sea; Day by day His sweet voice soundeth, Saying, "Christian, follow me!"

Jesus Calls Us

1. Jesus calls us o'er the tumult
   Of our life's wild, restless sea;
   Day by day His sweet voice soundeth,
   Saying, "Christian, follow Me!"

2. As of old the apostles heard it
   By the Galilean lake,
   Turned from home and toil and kindred,
   Leaving all for Jesus' sake.

3. Jesus calls us from the worship
   Of the vain world's golden store,
   From each idol that would keep us,
   Saying, "Christian, love Me more!"

4. In our joys and in our sorrows,
   Days of toil and hours of ease,
   Still He calls, in cares and pleasures,
   "Christian, love Me more than these!"

5. Jesus calls us: by Thy mercies,
   Savior, may we hear Thy call,
   Give our hearts to Thine obedience,
   Serve and love Thee best of all.

DISCIPLESHIP

61 Amazing Grace

AMAZING GRACE CM

Stanzas 1–4, John Newton, 1779
Stanza 5, *A Collection of Sacred Ballads,* 1790

Virginia Harmony, 1831
Arr. Edwin O. Excell, 1900

1. A-maz-ing grace! How sweet the sound That saved a wretch like me! I once was lost, but now am found, Was blind, but now I see.

Amazing Grace

1. Amazing grace! How sweet the sound
   That saved wretch like me!
   I once was lost, but now am found,
   Was blind, but now I see.

2. 'Twas grace that taught my heart to fear,
   And grace my fears relieved;
   How precious did that grace appear
   The hour I first believed!

3. Through many dangers, toils, and snares,
   I have already come;
   'Tis grace has brought me safe thus far,
   And grace will lead me home.

4. The Lord has promised good to me,
   His word my hope secures;
   He will my shield and portion be,
   As long as life endures.

5. When we've been there ten thousand years,
   Bright shining as the sun,
   We've no less days to sing God's praise
   Than when we'd first begun.

DISCIPLESHIP

62 Just as I Am, Without One Plea

WOODWORTH LM

Charlotte Elliot, 1834

William B. Bradbury, 1849

1. Just as I am with-out one plea, But that Thy blood was shed for me, And that Thou biddest me come to Thee, O Lamb of God, I come, I come!

Just as I Am, Without One Plea

1. Just as I am, without one plea,
   But that Thy blood was shed for me,
   And that Thou biddest me come to Thee,
   O Lamb of God, I come, I come!

2. Just as I am, though tossed about
   With many a conflict, many a doubt,
   Fightings and fears within, without,
   O Lamb of God, I come, I come!

3. Just as I am, Thou wilt receive,
   Wilt welcome, pardon, cleanse, relieve;
   Because Thy promise I believe,
   O Lamb of God, I come, I come!

4. Just as I am, Thy love unknown
   Has broken every barrier down;
   Now to be Thine, yea, Thine alone,
   O Lamb of God, I come, I come!

DISCIPLESHIP

63 Blessed Assurance, Jesus Is Mine!

ASSURANCE 9.10.9.9 with refrain

Fanny J. Crosby, 1873
Phoebe P. Knapp, 1873

1. Bless-ed as-sur-ance, Je-sus is mine! O what a fore-taste of glo-ry di-vine! Heir of sal-va-tion, pur-chase of God, Born of His Spir-it, washed in His blood.

Refrain
This is my sto-ry, this is my song, Prais-ing my Sav-ior all the day long. This is my sto-ry, this is my song, Prais-ing my Sav-ior all the day long.

Blessed Assurance, Jesus Is Mine!

63

1. Blessed assurance, Jesus is mine!
   O what a foretaste of glory divine!
   Heir of salvation, purchase of God,
   Born of His Spirit, washed in His blood.
   > This is my story, this is my song,
   > Praising my Savior all the day long.
   > This is my story, this is my song,
   > Praising my Savior all the day long.

2. Perfect submission, perfect delight,
   Visions of rapture now burst on my sight;
   Angels, descending, bring from above,
   Echoes of mercy, whispers of love.
   > This is my story, this is my song,
   > Praising my Savior all the day long.
   > This is my story, this is my song,
   > Praising my Savior all the day long.

3. Perfect submission, all is at rest,
   I in my Savior am happy and blest,
   Watching and waiting, looking above,
   Filled with His goodness, lost in His love.
   > This is my story, this is my song,
   > Praising my Savior all the day long.
   > This is my story, this is my song,
   > Praising my Savior all the day long.

DISCIPLESHIP

64 He Leadeth Me: O Blessed Thought!

HE LEADETH ME   LMD

Joseph H. Gilmore, 1862

William Bradbury, 1864

1. He leadeth me: O blessed thought! O words with heavenly comfort fraught! Whate'er I do, where'er I be, Still 'tis God's hand that leadeth me.

Refrain
He leadeth me, He leadeth me; By His own hand He leadeth me; His faithful follower I would be, For by His hand He leadeth me.

He Leadeth Me: O Blessed Thought!

1. He leadeth me: O blessed thought!
   O words with heavenly comfort fraught!
   Whate'er I do, where'er I be,
   Still 'tis God's hand that leadeth me.
   > He leadeth me, He leadeth me;
   > By His own hand He leadeth me;
   > His faithful follower I would be,
   > For by His hand He leadeth me.

2. Sometimes 'mid scenes of deepest gloom,
   Sometimes where Eden's bowers bloom,
   By waters still, o'er troubled sea,
   Still 'tis God's hand that leadeth me.
   > He leadeth me, He leadeth me;
   > By His own hand He leadeth me;
   > His faithful follower I would be,
   > For by His hand He leadeth me.

3. And when my task on earth is done,
   When, by Thy grace, the victory's won,
   E'en death's cold wave I will not flee,
   Since God through Jordan leadeth me.
   > He leadeth me, He leadeth me;
   > By His own hand He leadeth me;
   > His faithful follower I would be,
   > For by His hand He leadeth me.

DISCIPLESHIP

65 What a Friend We Have in Jesus

CONVERSE 8.7.8.7 D

Joseph M. Scriven, 1855

Charles C. Converse, 1868

1. What a friend we have in Jesus, All our sins and griefs to bear!
What a priv-i-lege to carry Ev-ery-thing to God in prayer!
O what peace we of-ten for-feit, O what need-less pain we bear,
All be-cause we do not carry Ev-ery-thing to God in prayer.

What a Friend We Have in Jesus

1. What a friend we have in Jesus,
   All our sins and griefs to bear!
   What a privilege to carry
   Everything to God in prayer!
   O what peace we often forfeit,
   O what needless pain we bear,
   All because we do not carry
   Everything to God in prayer!

2. Have we trials and temptations?
   Is there trouble anywhere?
   We should never be discouraged:
   Take it to the Lord in prayer!
   Can we find a friend so faithful,
   Who will all our sorrows share?
   Jesus knows our every weakness;
   Take it to the Lord in prayer!

3. Are we weak and heavy laden,
   Cumbered with a load of care?
   Precious Savior, still our refuge—
   Take it to the Lord in prayer!
   Do thy friends despise, forsake thee?
   Take it to the Lord in prayer!
   In His arms He'll take and shield thee,
   Thou wilt find a solace there.

DISCIPLESHIP

66 I Love to Tell the Story

I LOVE TO TELL THE STORY 7.6.7.6 D

Katherine Hankey, 1866 — William G. Fischer, 1869

1. I love to tell the story Of unseen things above, Of Jesus and His glory, Of Jesus and His love. I love to tell the story, Because I know 'tis true; It satisfies my longings As nothing else can do.

Refrain
I love to tell the story, 'Twill be my theme in glory To tell the old, old story Of Jesus and His love.

I Love to Tell the Story

1. I love to tell the story Of unseen things above,
   Of Jesus and His glory, Of Jesus and His love.
   I love to tell the story, Because I know 'tis true;
   It satisfies my longings As nothing else can do.
   > I love to tell the story,
   > 'Twill be my theme in glory,
   > To tell the old, old story
   > Of Jesus and His love.

2. I love to tell the story; More wonderful it seems
   Than all the golden fancies Of all our golden dreams,
   I love to tell the story, It did so much for me;
   And that is just the reason I tell it now to thee.
   > I love to tell the story,
   > 'Twill be my theme in glory,
   > To tell the old, old story
   > Of Jesus and His love.

3. I love to tell the story, For those who know it best
   Seem hungering and thirsting To hear it like the rest.
   And when, in scenes of glory, I sing the new, new song,
   'Twill be the old, old story That I have loved so long.
   > I love to tell the story,
   > 'Twill be my theme in glory,
   > To tell the old, old story
   > Of Jesus and His love.

DISCIPLESHIP

67 Stand Up, Stand Up for Jesus
WEBB 7.6.7.6 D

George Duffield, Jr., 1858

George J. Webb, 1837

1. Stand up, stand up for Jesus, Ye soldiers of the cross; Lift high His royal banner, It must not suffer loss: From victory unto victory His army shall He lead, Till every foe is vanquished, And Christ is Lord indeed.

Stand Up, Stand Up for Jesus

1. Stand up, stand up for Jesus,
   Ye soldiers of the cross;
   Lift high His royal banner,
   It must not suffer loss:
   From victory unto victory
   His army shall He lead,
   Till every foe is vanquished,
   And Christ is Lord indeed.

2. Stand up, stand up for Jesus,
   The trumpet call obey;
   Forth to the mighty conflict,
   In this His glorious day:
   Ye that are brave now serve Him
   Against unnumbered foes;
   Let courage rise with danger,
   And strength to strength oppose.

3. Stand up, stand up for Jesus,
   The strife will not be long;
   This day the noise of battle,
   The next, the victor's song:
   To him that overcometh,
   A crown of life shall be;
   He with the King of Glory
   Shall reign eternally.

DISCIPLESHIP

68 Onward, Christian Soldiers

ST. GERTRUDE   6.5.6.5 D with refrain

Sabine Baring-Gould, 1865; alt.   Arthur S. Sullivan, 1871

1. Onward, Christian soldiers, Marching as to war,
With the cross of Jesus Going on before.
Christ, the royal Master, Leads against the foe;
Forward into battle See His banners go!

Refrain
Onward, Christian soldiers, Marching as to war,
With the cross of Jesus Going on before.

Onward, Christian Soldiers

1. Onward, Christian soldiers, marching as to war,
   With the cross of Jesus going on before.
   Christ, the royal Master, leads against the foe;
   Forward into battle, see His banners go!
   > Onward, Christian soldiers, marching as to war,
   > With the cross of Jesus going on before.

2. Like a mighty army moves the church of God;
   Christians, we are treading where the saints have trod;
   We are not divided, all one body we,
   One in hope and doctrine, one in charity.
   > Onward, Christian soldiers, marching as to war,
   > With the cross of Jesus going on before.

3. Onward, then, ye people, join our happy throng,
   Blend with ours your voices in the triumph song;
   Glory, laud, and honor unto Christ the King;
   This through countless ages we with angels sing.
   > Onward, Christian soldiers, marching as to war,
   > With the cross of Jesus going on before.

DISCIPLESHIP

69 Faith of Our Fathers

ST. CATHERINE 8.8.8.8.8.8

Frederick W. Faber, 1849

Henri F. Hemy, 1865; alt.

1. Faith of our fathers! living still In spite of dungeon, fire, and sword; O how our hearts beat high with joy When-e'er we hear that glorious word! Faith of our fathers, holy faith! We will be true to thee till death.

Faith of Our Fathers

1. Faith of our fathers! living still
   In spite of dungeon, fire, and sword;
   O how our hearts beat high with joy
   Whene'er we hear that glorious word!
      Faith of our fathers, holy faith!
      We will be true to thee till death.

2. Faith of our fathers! we will strive
   To win all nations unto thee,
   And through the truth that comes from God
   Mankind shall then be truly free.
      Faith of our fathers, holy faith!
      We will be true to thee till death.

3. Faith of our fathers! we will love
   Both friend and foe in all our strife,
   And preach thee, too, as love knows how
   By kindly words and virtuous life:
      Faith of our fathers, holy faith!
      We will be true to thee till death.

DISCIPLESHIP
70 My Faith Looks Up to Thee

OLIVET 6.6.4.6.6.6.4

Ray Palmer, 1830 — Lowell Mason, 1831

1. My faith looks up to Thee, Thou Lamb of Calvary, Savior divine: Now hear me while I pray, Take all my guilt away, O let me from this day Be wholly Thine!

My Faith Looks Up to Thee

1. My faith looks up to Thee,
   Thou Lamb of Calvary,
   Savior divine:
   Now hear me while I pray,
   Take all my guilt away,
   O let me from this day
   Be wholly Thine!

2. May Thy rich grace impart
   Strength to my fainting heart,
   My zeal inspire;
   As Thou hast died for me,
   O may my love to Thee
   Pure, warm, and changeless be,
   A living fire!

3. When ends life's transient dream,
   When death's cold, sullen stream
   Shall o'er me roll,
   Blest Savior, then, in love,
   Fear and distrust remove;
   O bear me safe above,
   A ransomed soul!

DISCIPLESHIP
71

Jesus Loves Me!

JESUS LOVES ME   7.7.7.7 with refrain

Anna Warner, 1859

William B. Bradbury, 1861

1. Jesus loves me! this I know, For the Bible tells me so;
Little ones to Him belong; They are weak, but He is strong.

Refrain
Yes, Jesus loves me! Yes, Jesus loves me!
Yes, Jesus loves me! The Bible tells me so.

Jesus Loves Me!

1. Jesus loves me! This I know,
   For the Bible tells me so;
   Little ones to Him belong;
   They are weak, but He is strong.
   > Yes, Jesus loves me!
   > Yes, Jesus loves me!
   > Yes, Jesus loves me!
   > The Bible tells me so.

2. Jesus loves me! This I know,
   As He loved so long ago,
   Taking children on his knee,
   Saying, "Let them come to Me."
   > Yes, Jesus loves me!
   > Yes, Jesus loves me!
   > Yes, Jesus loves me!
   > The Bible tells me so.

DISCIPLESHIP

72 Love Divine, All Loves Excelling

BEECHER 8.7.8.7 D

Charles Wesley, 1747

John Zundel, 1870

1. Love divine, all loves excelling, Joy of heaven, to earth come down,
Fix in us Thy humble dwelling, All Thy faithful mercies crown!
Jesus, Thou art all compassion, Pure, unbounded love Thou art;
Visit us with Thy salvation, Enter every trembling heart.

Love Divine, All Loves Excelling

1. Love divine, all loves excelling,
   Joy of heaven, to earth come down,
   Fix in us Thy humble dwelling,
   All Thy faithful mercies crown!
   Jesus, Thou art all compassion,
   Pure, unbounded love Thou art;
   Visit us with Thy salvation,
   Enter every trembling heart.

2. Breathe, O breathe Thy loving Spirit
   Into every troubled breast!
   Let us all in Thee inherit,
   Let us find the promised rest;
   Take away the love of sinning;
   Alpha and Omega be;
   End of faith, as its beginning,
   Set our hearts at liberty.

3. Finish, then, Thy new creation;
   Pure and spotless let us be;
   Let us see Thy great salvation
   Perfectly restored in Thee;
   Changed from glory into glory,
   Till in heaven we take our place,
   Till we cast our crowns before Thee,
   Lost in wonder, love, and praise.

DISCIPLESHIP

73 Immortal Love, Forever Full
SERENITY CM

John Greenleaf Whittier, 1866

Arr. from William V. Wallace, 1856

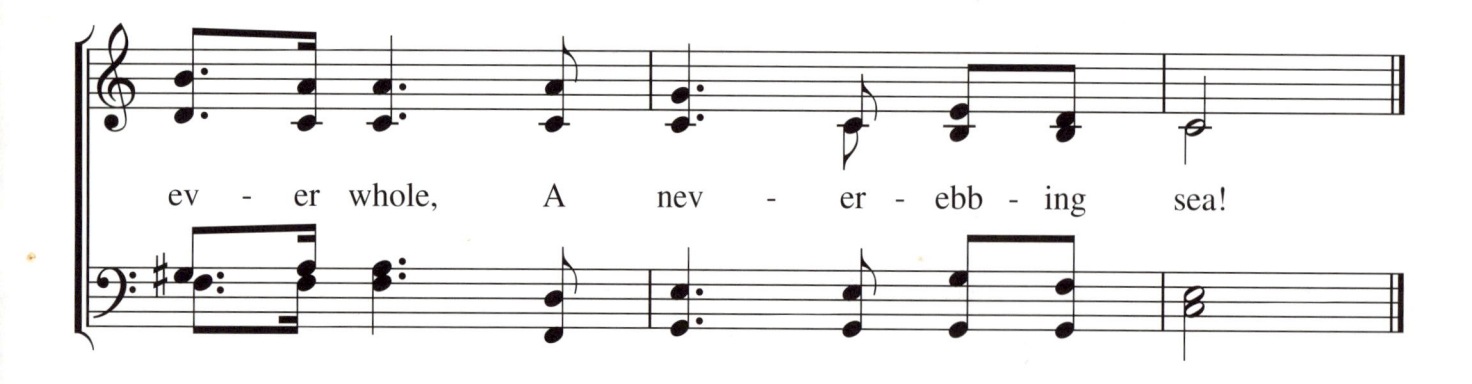

1. Immortal Love, forever full, Forever flowing free, Forever shared, forever whole, A never-ebbing sea!

Immortal Love, Forever Full

1. Immortal Love, forever full,
   Forever flowing free,
   Forever shared, forever whole,
   A never-ebbing sea!

2. We may not climb the heavenly steeps
   To bring the Lord Christ down;
   In vain we search the lowest deeps,
   For Him no depths can drown.

3. The healing of His seamless dress
   Is by our beds of pain;
   We touch Him in life's throng and press,
   And we are whole again.

4. Through Him the first fond prayers are said,
   Our lips of childhood frame;
   The last low whispers of our dead
   Are burdened with His name.

5. O Lord and Master of us all:
   Whate'er our name or sign,
   We own Thy sway, we hear Thy call,
   We test our lives by Thine!

DISCIPLESHIP

74 O Love That Wilt Not Let Me Go

ST. MARGARET 8.8.8.8.6

George Matheson, 1882 Albert Lister Peace, 1884

1. O love that wilt not let me go, I rest my weary soul in Thee; I give Thee back the life I owe, That in Thine ocean depths its flow May richer, fuller be.

O Love That Wilt Not Let Me Go

DISCIPLESHIP
74

1. O love that wilt not let me go,
   I rest my weary soul in Thee;
   I give Thee back the life I owe,
   That in Thine ocean depths its flow
   May richer, fuller be.

2. O light that followest all my way,
   I yield my flickering torch to Thee;
   My heart restores its borrowed ray,
   That in Thy sunshine's blaze its day
   May brighter, fairer be.

3. O joy that seekest me through pain,
   I cannot close my heart to Thee;
   I trace the rainbow through the rain,
   And feel the promise is not vain
   That morn shall tearless be.

4. O cross that liftest up my head,
   I dare not ask to fly from Thee;
   I lay in dust life's glory dead,
   And from the ground there blossoms red
   Life that shall endless be.

DISCIPLESHIP

75 Rock of Ages, Cleft for Me

TOPLADY 7.7.7.7.7.7

Augustus M. Toplady, 1776; alt.
Thomas Hastings, 1830

1. Rock of Ages, cleft for me, Let me hide myself in Thee; Let the water and the blood, From Thy wounded side which flowed, Be of sin the double cure, Save from wrath and make me pure.

Rock of Ages, Cleft for Me

1. Rock of Ages, cleft for me,
   Let me hide myself in Thee;
   Let the water and the blood,
   From Thy wounded side which flowed,
   Be of sin the double cure,
   Save from wrath and make me pure.

2. Could my tears forever flow,
   Could my zeal no languor know
   These for sin could not atone;
   Thou must save, and Thou alone,
   In my hand no price I bring;
   Simply to Thy cross I cling.

3. While I draw this fleeting breath,
   When my eyes shall close in death,
   When I rise to worlds unknown,
   And behold Thee on Thy throne,
   Rock of Ages, cleft for me,
   Let me hide myself in Thee.

DISCIPLESHIP

76 Jesus, Savior, Pilot Me

PILOT 7.7.7.7.7.7

Edward Hopper, 1871

John E. Gould, 1871

1. Jesus, Savior, pilot me
Over life's tempestuous sea;
Unknown waves before me roll,
Hiding rock and treacherous shoal;
Chart and compass came from Thee:
Jesus, Savior, pilot me.

Jesus, Savior, Pilot Me

1. Jesus, Savior, pilot me
   Over life's tempestuous sea;
   Unknown waves before me roll,
   Hiding rock and treacherous shoal;
   Chart and compass came from Thee:
   Jesus, Savior, pilot me.

2. As a mother stills her child,
   Thou canst hush the ocean wild;
   Boisterous waves obey Thy will
   When Thou sayest to them, "Be still!"
   Wondrous Sovereign of the sea,
   Jesus, Savior, pilot me.

3. When at last I near the shore,
   And the fearful breakers roar
   'Twixt me and the peaceful rest,
   Then, while leaning on Thy breast,
   May I hear Thee say to me,
   "Fear not, I will pilot thee."

DISCIPLESHIP

77 Savior, Like a Shepherd Lead Us

BRADBURY   8.7.8.7 D

Hymns for the Young, 1836
Attr. Dorothy A. Thrupp (1779–1847)

William B. Bradbury, 1859

1. Savior, like a shepherd lead us, Much we need Thy tender care; In Thy pleasant pastures feed us, For our use Thy folds prepare; Blessed Jesus, blessed Jesus, Thou hast bought us, Thine we are; Blessed Jesus, blessed Jesus, Thou hast bought us, Thine we are.

Savior, Like a Shepherd Lead Us

1. Savior, like a shepherd lead us,
   Much we need Thy tender care;
   In Thy pleasant pastures feed us,
   For our use Thy folds prepare;
   Blessed Jesus, blessed Jesus,
   Thou hast bought us, Thine we are;
   Blessed Jesus, blessed Jesus,
   Thou hast bought us, Thine we are.

2. Thou hast promised to receive us,
   Poor and sinful though we be;
   Thou hast mercy to relieve us,
   Grace to cleanse, and power to free:
   Blessed Jesus, blessed Jesus,
   Early let us turn to Thee;
   Blessed Jesus, blessed Jesus,
   Early let us turn to Thee.

3. Early let us seek Thy favor;
   Early let us do Thy will;
   Blessed Lord and only Savior,
   With Thy love our bosoms fill:
   Blessed Jesus, blessed Jesus,
   Thou hast loved us, love us still;
   Blessed Jesus, blessed Jesus,
   Thou hast loved us, love us still.

DISCIPLESHIP

78 Come, Thou Fount of Every Blessing

NETTLETON 8.7.8.7 D

Robert Robinson, c. 1758

Wyeth's *Repository of Sacred Music*, 1813

1. Come, Thou Fount of every blessing, Tune my heart to sing Thy grace; Streams of mercy, never ceasing, Call for songs of loudest praise. Teach me some melodious sonnet, Sung by flaming tongues above; Praise the mount! I'm fixed upon it, Mount of God's unchanging love.

Come, Thou Fount of Every Blessing

1. Come, Thou Fount of every blessing,
   Tune my heart to sing Thy grace;
   Streams of mercy, never ceasing,
   Call for songs of loudest praise.
   Teach me some melodious sonnet,
   Sung by flaming tongues above;
   Praise the mount! I'm fixed upon it,
   Mount of God's unchanging love.

2. Here I raise my Ebenezer,
   Hither by Thy help I'm come;
   And I hope, by Thy good pleasure,
   Safely to arrive at home.
   Jesus sought me when a stranger,
   Wandering from the fold of God;
   He, to rescue me from danger,
   Interposed His precious blood.

3. O to grace how great a debtor
   Daily I'm constrained to be!
   Let that grace now, like a fetter,
   Bind my wandering heart to Thee:
   Prone to wander, Lord, I feel it,
   Prone to leave the God I love;
   Here's my heart, O take and seal it,
   Seal it for Thy courts above.

DISCIPLESHIP

79 O for a Closer Walk with God

DALEHURST CM

William Cowper, 1772

Arthur Cottman, 1874

1. O for a closer walk with God, A calm and heavenly frame, A light to shine upon the road That leads me to the Lamb!

O for a Closer Walk with God

1. O for a closer walk with God,
   A calm and heavenly frame,
   A light to shine upon the road
   That leads me to the Lamb!

2. Return, O holy Dove, return,
   Sweet messenger of rest!
   I hate the sins that made Thee mourn
   And drove Thee from my breast.

3. The dearest idol I have known,
   Whate'er that idol be,
   Help me to tear it from Thy throne,
   And worship only Thee.

4. So shall my walk be close with God,
   Calm and serene my frame;
   So purer light shall mark the road
   That leads me to the Lamb.

DISCIPLESHIP

80 Jesus, the Very Thought of Thee

ST. AGNES   CM

Attr. Bernard of Clairvaux
Trans. Edward Caswall, 1849; alt. 1987

John B. Dykes, 1866

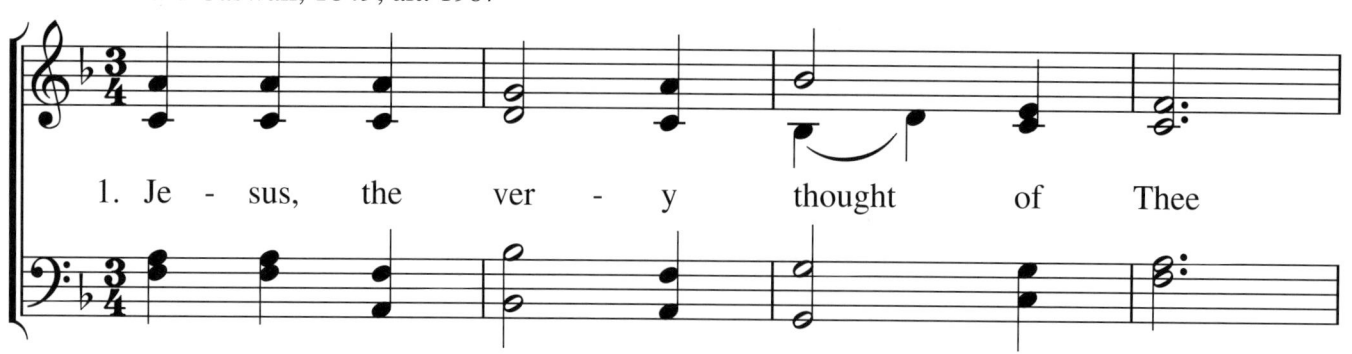

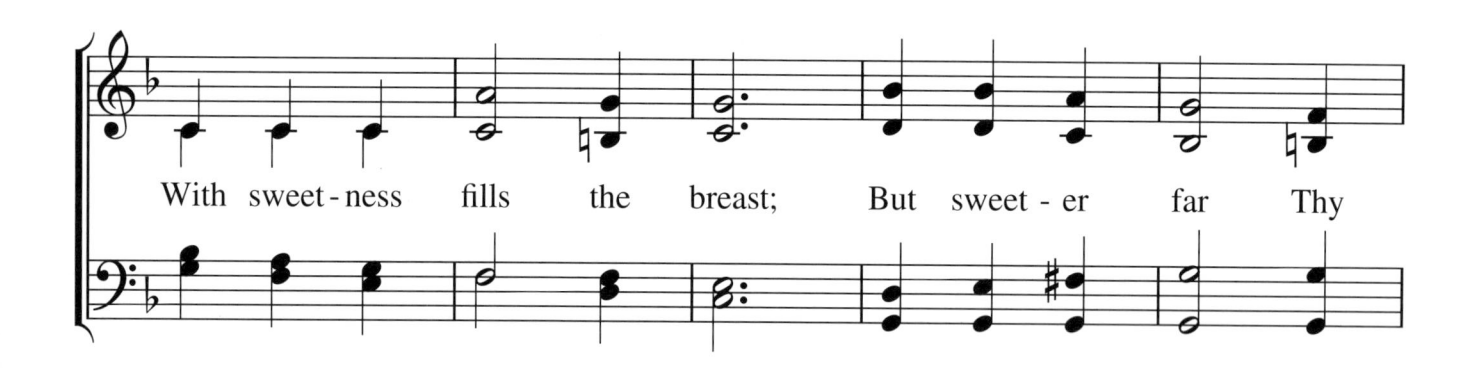

1. Jesus, the very thought of Thee
With sweetness fills the breast;
But sweeter far Thy face to see,
And in Thy presence rest.

Jesus, the Very Thought of Thee

1. Jesus, the very thought of Thee
   With sweetness fills the breast;
   But sweeter far Thy face to see,
   And in Thy presence rest.

2. Nor voice can sing, nor heart can frame,
   Nor can the mind recall
   A sweeter sound than Thy blest name,
   O Savior of us all.

3. O hope of every contrite heart,
   O joy of all the meek,
   To those who fall, how kind Thou art!
   How good to those who seek!

4. But what to those who find? Ah, this
   Nor tongue nor pen can show:
   The love of Jesus, what it is
   None but His loved ones know.

5. Jesus, our only joy be Thou,
   As Thou our prize wilt be;
   Jesus, be Thou our glory now,
   And through eternity.

DISCIPLESHIP

81 Guide Me, O Thou Great Jehovah

CWM RHONDDA   8.7.8.7.8.7.7

William Williams, 1745
Stanza 1 trans. Peter Williams, 1771
Stanzas 2–3 trans. William Williams, 1772

John Hughes, 1907

1. Guide me, O Thou great Jehovah, Pilgrim through this barren land; I am weak, but Thou art mighty; Hold me with Thy powerful hand; Bread of heaven, bread of heaven, Feed me till I want no more, Feed me till I want no more.

Guide Me, O Thou Great Jehovah

1. Guide me, O Thou great Jehovah,
   Pilgrim through this barren land;
   I am weak, but Thou art mighty;
   Hold me with Thy powerful hand;
   Bread of heaven, bread of heaven,
   Feed me till I want no more,
   Feed me till I want no more.

2. Open now the crystal fountain,
   Whence the healing stream doth flow;
   Let the fire and cloudy pillar
   Lead me all my journey through;
   Strong deliverer, strong deliverer,
   Be Thou still my strength and shield,
   Be Thou still my strength and shield.

3. When I tread the verge of Jordan,
   Bid my anxious fears subside;
   Death of death, and hell's destruction,
   Land me safe on Canaan's side;
   Songs of praises, songs of praises
   I will ever give to Thee,
   I will ever give to Thee.

DISCIPLESHIP
82
Lead On, O King Eternal
LANCASHIRE   7.6.7.6 D

Ernest W. Shurtleff, 1888

Henry Smart, c. 1835

1. Lead on, O King e-ter-nal, The day of march has come; Hence-forth in fields of con-quest Thy tents shall be our home: Through days of prep-a-ra-tion Thy grace has made us strong, And now, O King e-ter-nal, We lift our bat-tle song.

Lead On, O King Eternal

1. Lead on, O King eternal,
   The day of march has come;
   Henceforth in fields of conquest
   Thy tents shall be our home:
   Through days of preparation
   Thy grace has made us strong,
   And now, O King eternal,
   We lift our battle song.

2. Lead on, O King eternal,
   Till sin's fierce war shall cease,
   And holiness shall whisper
   The sweet amen of peace;
   For not with swords' loud clashing,
   Nor roll of stirring drums;
   With deeds of love and mercy
   The heavenly kingdom comes.

3. Lead on, O King eternal:
   We follow, not with fears,
   For gladness breaks like morning,
   Where'er Thy face appears;
   Thy cross is lifted o'er us;
   We journey in its light:
   The crown awaits the conquest;
   Lead on, O God of might.

DISCIPLESHIP

83 O Master, Let Me Walk with Thee

MARYTON LM

Washington Gladden, 1879

Henry Percy Smith, 1874

1. O Master, let me walk with Thee In lowly paths of service free; Tell me Thy secret; help me bear The strain of toil, the fret of care.

O Master, Let Me Walk with Thee

1. O Master, let me walk with Thee
   In lowly paths of service free;
   Tell me Thy secret; help me bear
   The strain of toil, the fret of care.

2. Help me the slow of heart to move
   By some clear, winning word of love;
   Teach me the wayward feet to stay,
   And guide them in the homeward way.

3. Teach me Thy patience; still with Thee
   In closer, dearer company,
   In work that keeps faith sweet and strong,
   In trust that triumphs over wrong.

4. In hope that sends a shining ray
   Far down the future's broadening way;
   In peace that only Thou canst give,
   With Thee, O Master, let me live.

DISCIPLESHIP
84
Lord, I Want to Be a Christian

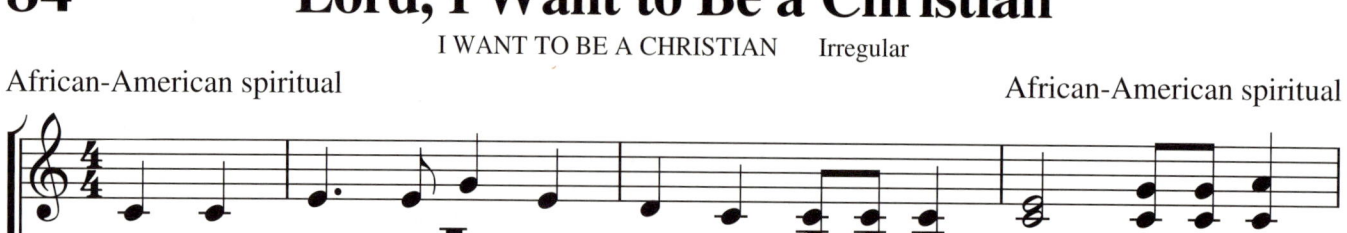

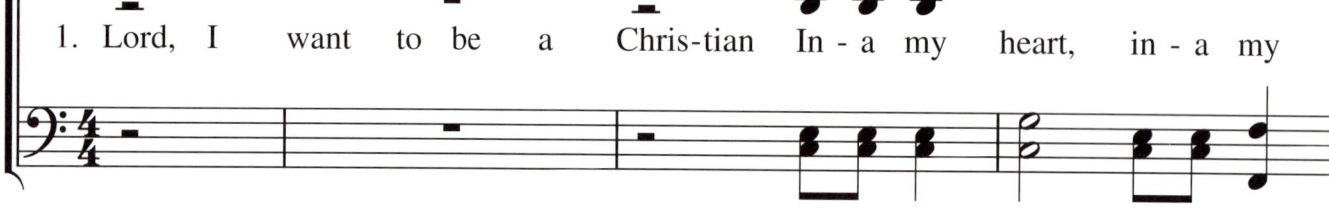

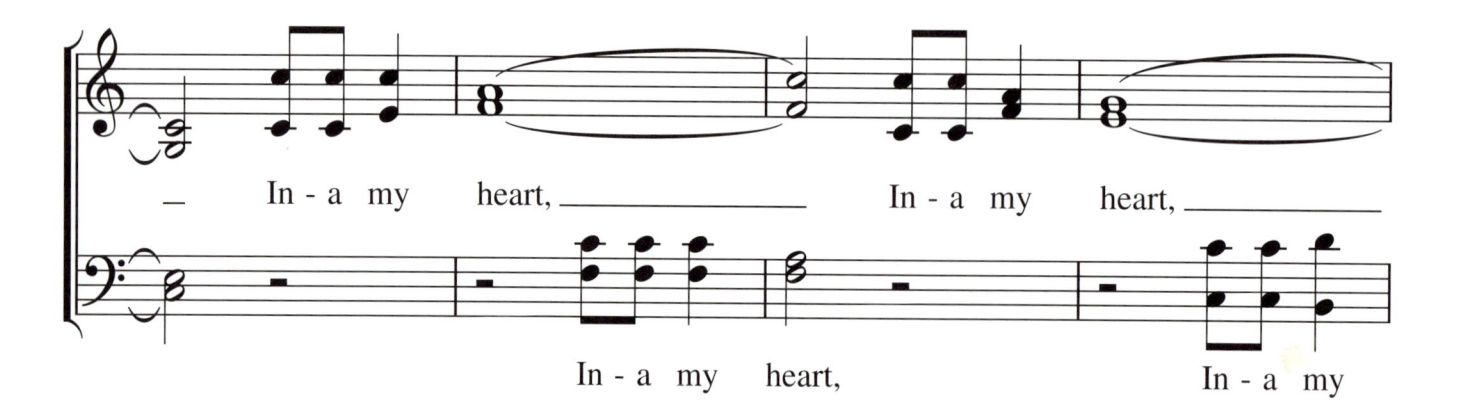

I WANT TO BE A CHRISTIAN   Irregular

African-American spiritual   African-American spiritual

1. Lord, I want to be a Christian In-a my heart, in-a my heart, Lord, I want to be a Christian In-a my heart. In-a my heart, In-a my heart, In-a my heart, In-a my Lord, I want to be a Christian In-a my heart. heart,

Lord, I Want to Be a Christian

1. Lord, I want to be a Christian
   In-a my heart, in-a my heart,
   Lord, I want to be Christian
   In-a my heart.
   In-a my heart, in-a my heart,
   Lord, I want to be a Christian
   In-a my heart.

2. Lord, I want to be more loving
   In-a my heart, in-a my heart,
   Lord, I want to be more loving
   In-a my heart.
   In-a my heart, in-a my heart,
   Lord, I want to be more loving
   In-a my heart.

3. (Lord, I want to be more holy)

4. Lord, I want to be like Jesus
   In-a my heart, in-a my heart,
   Lord, I want to be like Jesus
   In-a my heart.
   In-a my heart, in-a my heart,
   Lord, I want to be like Jesus
   In-a my heart.

DISCIPLESHIP

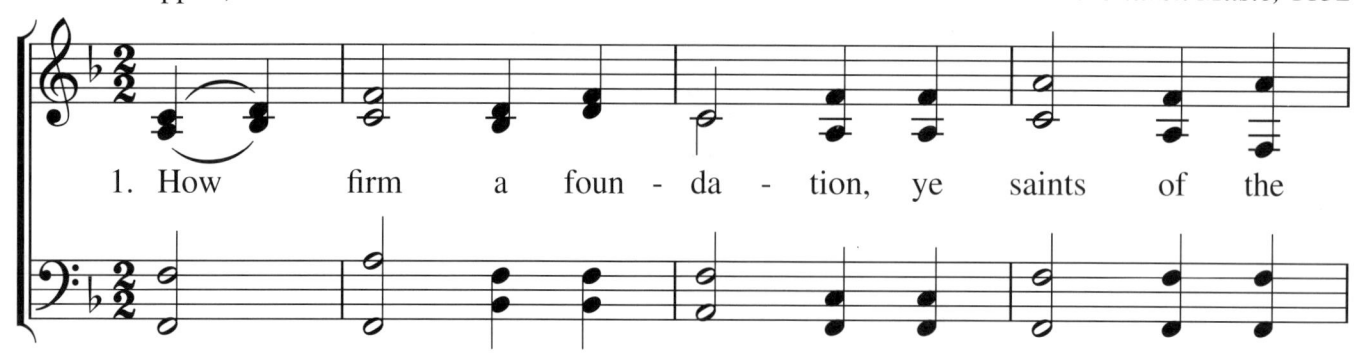

85 How Firm a Foundation

FOUNDATION 11.11.11.11

"K" in *A Selection of Hymns*, 1787
Ed. John Rippon; alt.

American Folk melody
Funk's *Genuine Church Music*, 1832

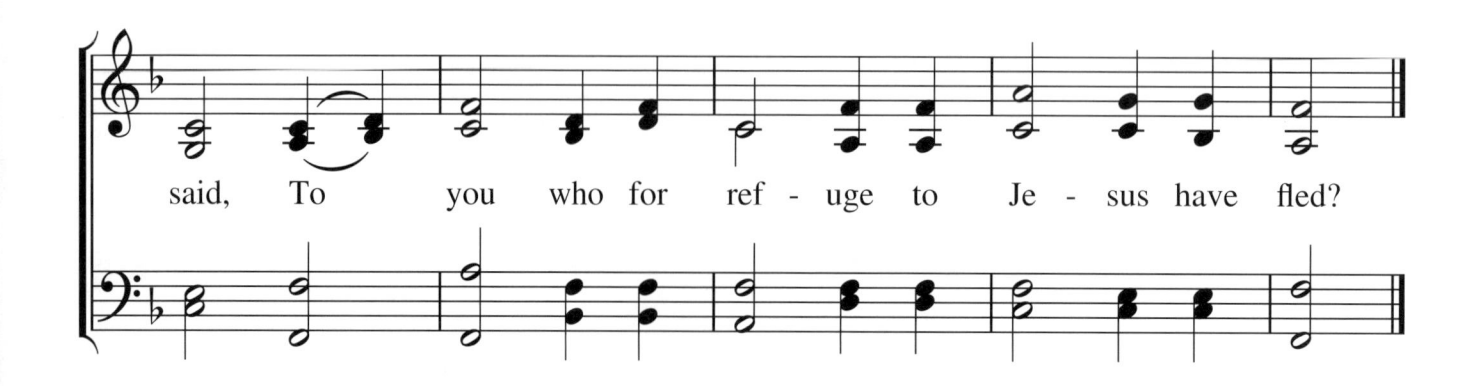

1. How firm a foundation, ye saints of the Lord, Is laid for your faith in God's excellent Word! What more can be said than to you God hath said, To you who for refuge to Jesus have fled?

How Firm a Foundation

1. How firm a foundation, ye saints of the Lord,
   Is laid for your faith in God's excellent Word!
   What more can be said than to you God hath said,
   To you who for refuge to Jesus have fled?

2. "Fear not, I am with thee, O be not dismayed,
   For I am thy God, and will still give thee aid;
   I'll strengthen thee, help thee, and cause thee to stand,
   Upheld by My righteous, omnipotent hand.

3. "When through the deep waters I call thee to go,
   The rivers of sorrow shall not overflow;
   For I will be near thee, thy troubles to bless,
   And sanctify to thee thy deepest distress.

4. "When through fiery trials thy pathway shall lie,
   My grace, all-sufficient, shall be thy supply;
   The flame shall not hurt thee; I only design
   Thy dross to consume, and thy gold to refine.

5. "The soul that on Jesus hath leaned for repose,
   I will not, I will not desert to its foes;
   That soul, though all hell should endeavor to shake,
   I'll never, no, never, no, never forsake."

DISCIPLINESHIP

86

Take My Life

HENDON 7.7.7.7

Frances Ridley Havergal, 1874

H. A. César Malan, 1827

1. Take my life, and let it be Con-se-crat-ed, Lord, to Thee. Take my mo-ments and my days; Let them flow in cease-less praise, Let them flow in cease-less praise.

Take My Life

1. Take my life, and let it be
   Consecrated, Lord, to Thee.
   Take my moments and my days;
   Let them flow in ceaseless praise,
   Let them flow in ceaseless praise.

2. Take my voice, and let me sing,
   Always, only, for my King.
   Take my lips, and let them be
   Filled with messages from Thee,
   Filled with messages from Thee.

3. Take my silver and my gold,
   Not a mite would I withhold;
   Take my intellect, and use
   Every power as Thou shalt choose,
   Every power as Thou shalt choose.

4. Take my love; my Lord, I pour
   At Thy feet its treasure store.
   Take myself, and I will be
   Ever, only, all for Thee,
   Ever, only, all for Thee.

DISCIPLESHIP

87 We Give Thee but Thine Own

SCHUMANN SM

William Walsham How, c. 1858

Mason and Webb's *Cantica Laudis,* 1850

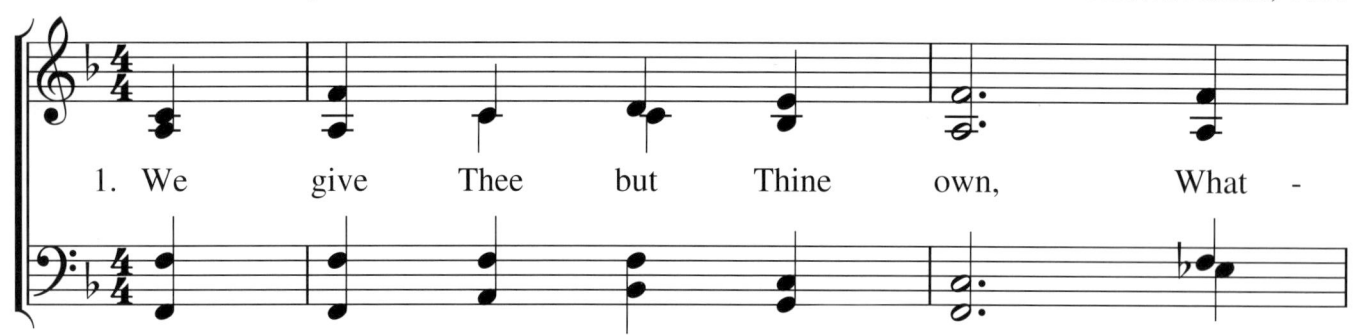

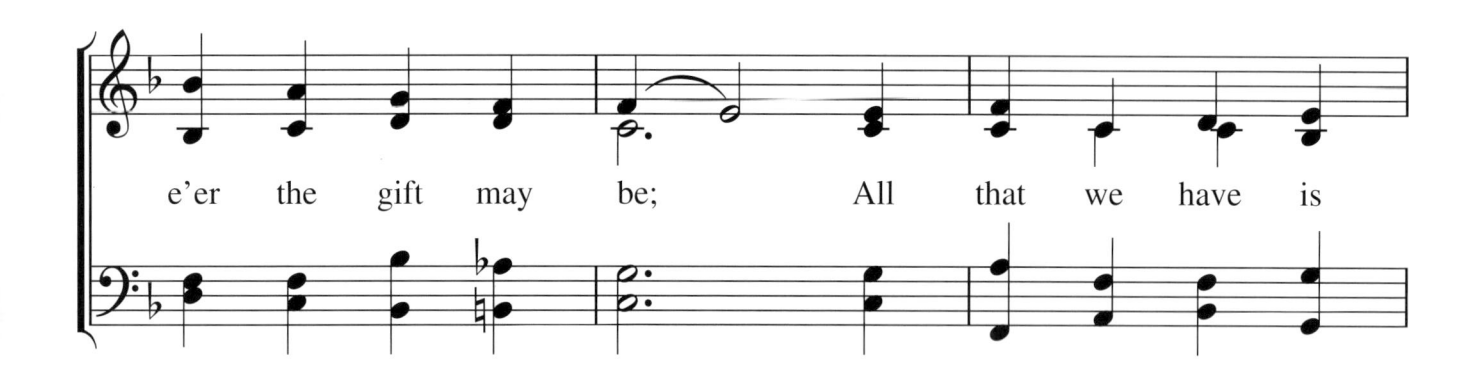

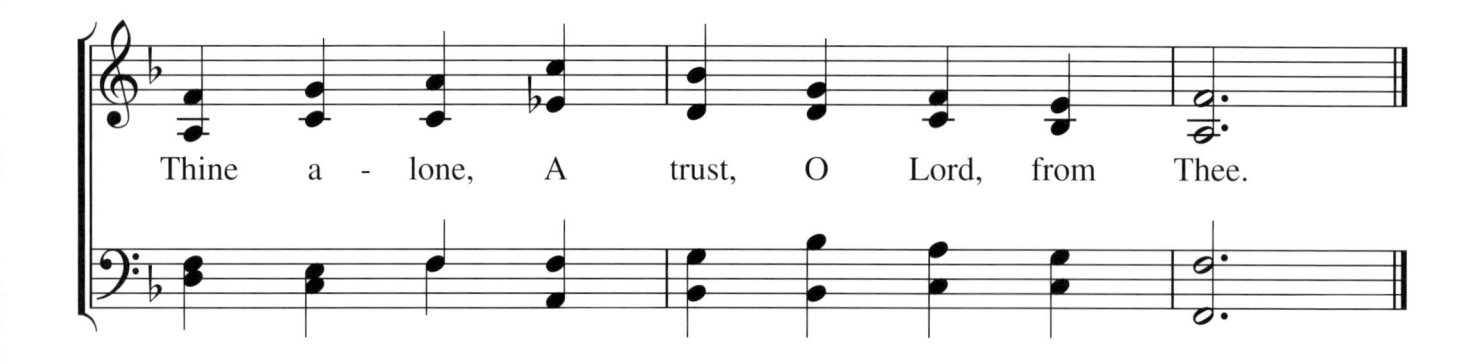

1. We give Thee but Thine own, What-e'er the gift may be; All that we have is Thine alone, A trust, O Lord, from Thee.

We Give Thee but Thine Own

DISCIPLESHIP 87

1. We give Thee but Thine own,
   Whate'er the gift may be;
   All that we have is Thine alone,
   A trust, O Lord, from Thee.

2. May we Thy bounties thus
   As stewards true receive,
   And gladly, as Thou blessest us,
   To Thee our firstfruits give.

3. To comfort and to bless,
   To find a balm for woe,
   To tend the lonely in distress,
   Is angels' work below.

4. The captive to release,
   To God the lost to bring,
   To teach the way of life and peace—
   It is a Christlike thing.

5. And we believe Thy Word,
   Though dim our faith may be;
   Whate'er for Thine we do, O Lord,
   We do it unto Thee.

DISCIPLESHIP

88 There's a Wideness in God's Mercy

IN BABILONE 8.7.8.7 D

Frederick William Faber, 1854; alt.

Dutch melody
Arr. Julius Röntgen, 1855–1933

1. There's a wide-ness in God's mer-cy Like the wide-ness of the sea;
There's a kind-ness in God's jus-tice, Which is more than lib-er-ty.
There is no place where earth's sor-rows Are more felt than up in heaven;
There is no place where earth's fail-ings Have such kind-ly judg-ment given.

There's a Wideness in God's Mercy

1. There's a wideness in God's mercy
   Like the wideness of the sea;
   There's a kindness in God's justice,
   Which is more than liberty.
   There is no place where earth's sorrows
   Are more felt than up in heaven;
   There is no place where earth's failings
   Have such kindly judgment given.

2. For the love of God is broader
   Than the measures of the mind;
   And the heart of the Eternal
   Is most wonderfully kind.
   If our love were but more faithful,
   We would gladly trust God's Word;
   And our lives reflect thanksgiving
   For the goodness of our Lord.

DISCIPLESHIP

89 O Jesus, I Have Promised

ANGEL'S STORY 7.6.7.6 D

John Ernest Bode, 1866　　　　　　　　　　　　　　　　　Arthur Henry Mann, 1881

1. O Jesus I have promised To serve Thee to the end; Be Thou forever near me, My Master and my friend; I shall not fear the battle If Thou art by my side, Nor wander from the pathway If Thou wilt be my guide.

O Jesus, I Have Promised

1. O Jesus I have promised
   To serve Thee to the end;
   Be Thou forever near me,
   My Master and my friend;
   I shall not fear the battle
   If Thou art by my side,
   Nor wander from the pathway
   If Thou wilt be my guide.

2. O let me hear Thee speaking
   In accents clear and still,
   Above the storms of passion,
   The murmurs of self-will;
   O speak to reassure me,
   To hasten or control;
   O speak, and make me listen,
   Thou guardian of my soul.

3. O Jesus, Thou hast promised
   To all who follow Thee
   That where Thou art in glory
   There shall Thy servant be;
   And, Jesus, I have promised
   To serve Thee to the end;
   O give me grace to follow,
   My Master and my friend.

DISCIPLESHIP

90 Where Cross the Crowded Ways of Life
GERMANY LM

Frank M. North, 1905; alt.

Attr. Ludwig van Beethoven (1770–1827)
Gardiner's *Sacred Melodies*, 1815

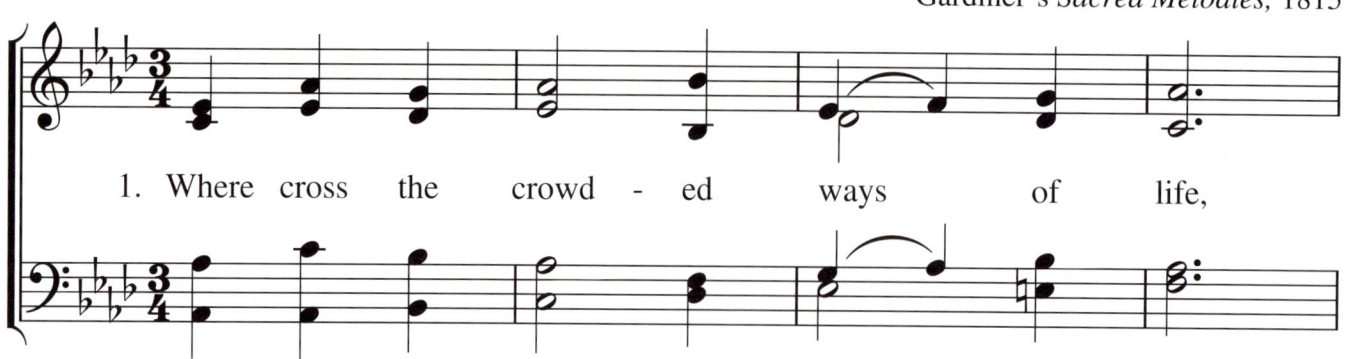

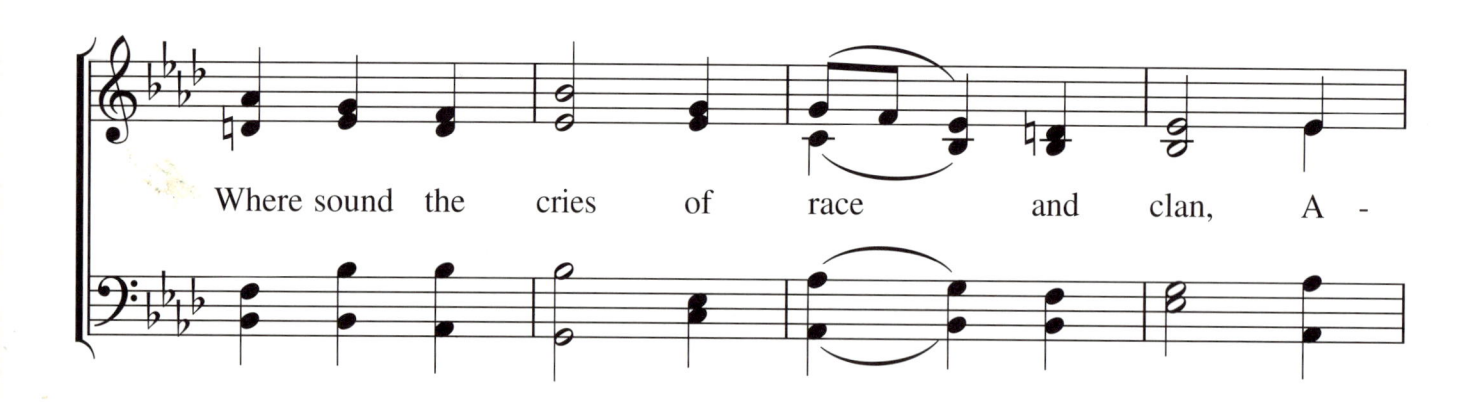

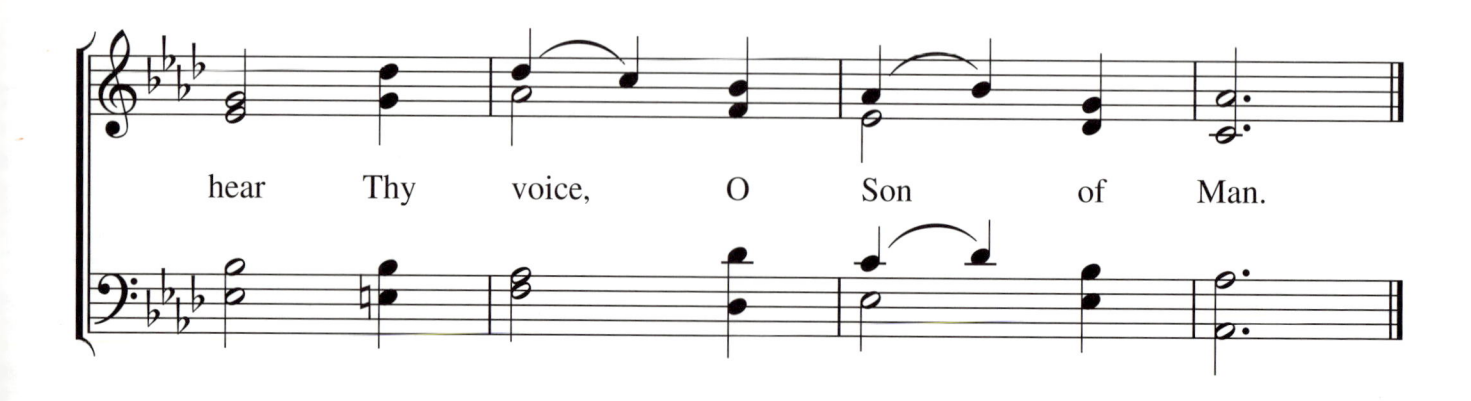

1. Where cross the crowded ways of life, Where sound the cries of race and clan, Above the noise of selfish strife, We hear Thy voice, O Son of Man.

Where Cross the Crowded Ways of Life

1. Where cross the crowded ways of life,
   Where sound the cries of race and clan,
   Above the noise of selfish strife,
   We hear Thy voice, O Son of Man.

2. In haunts of wretchedness and need,
   On shadowed thresholds fraught with fears,
   From paths where hide the lures of greed,
   We catch the vision of Thy tears.

3. From tender childhood's helplessness,
   From human grief and burdened toil,
   From famished souls, from sorrow's stress,
   Thy heart has never known recoil.

4. The cup of water given for Thee
   Still holds the freshness of Thy grace;
   Yet long these multitudes to see
   The sweet compassion of Thy face.

5. Till all the world shall learn Thy love,
   And follow where Thy feet have trod;
   Till glorious from Thy heaven above
   Shall come the city of our God.

PRAYER

91 There Is a Place of Quiet Rest

McAFEE   CM with refrain

Cleland B. McAfee, 1901   Cleland B. McAfee, 1901

1. There is a place of qui-et rest, Near to the heart of God, A place where sin can-not mo-lest, Near to the heart of God.

Refrain

O Je-sus, blest Re-deem-er, Sent from the heart of God, Hold us, who wait be-fore Thee, Near to the heart of God.

There Is a Place of Quiet Rest

PRAYER 91

1. There is a place of quiet rest,
   Near to the heart of God,
   A place where sin cannot molest,
   Near to the heart of God.
   > O Jesus, blest Redeemer,
   > Sent from the heart of God,
   > Hold us, who wait before Thee,
   > Near to the heart of God.

2. There is a place of comfort sweet,
   Near to the heart of God,
   A place where we our Savior meet,
   Near to the heart of God.
   > O Jesus, blest Redeemer,
   > Sent from the heart of God,
   > Hold us, who wait before Thee,
   > Near to the heart of God.

3. There is a place of full release,
   Near to the heart of God,
   A place where all is joy and peace,
   Near to the heart of God.
   > O Jesus, blest Redeemer,
   > Sent from the heart of God,
   > Hold us, who wait before Thee,
   > Near to the heart of God.

PRAYER

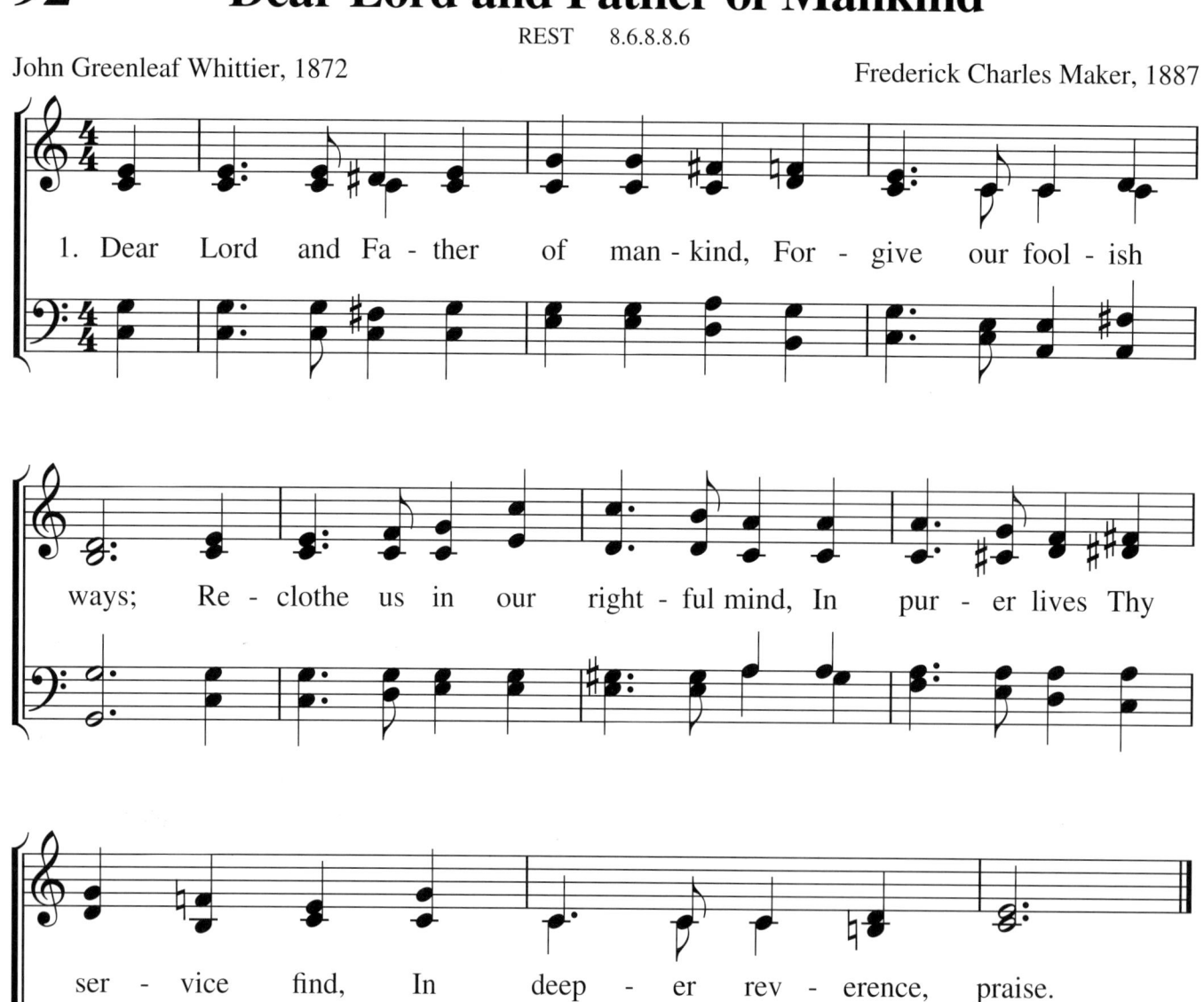

92 Dear Lord and Father of Mankind

REST 8.6.8.8.6

John Greenleaf Whittier, 1872

Frederick Charles Maker, 1887

1. Dear Lord and Father of mankind, Forgive our foolish ways; Re-clothe us in our rightful mind, In purer lives Thy service find, In deeper reverence, praise.

Dear Lord and Father of Mankind

PRAYER 92

1. Dear Lord and Father of mankind,
   Forgive our foolish ways;
   Reclothe us in our rightful mind,
   In purer lives Thy service find,
   In deeper reverence, praise.

2. In simple trust like theirs who heard,
   Beside the Syrian sea,
   The gracious calling of the Lord,
   Let us, like them, without a word
   Rise up and follow Thee.

3. Drop Thy still dews of quietness,
   Till all our strivings cease;
   Take from our souls the strain and stress,
   And let our ordered lives confess
   The beauty of Thy peace.

4. Breathe through the heats of our desire
   Thy coolness and Thy balm;
   Let sense be dumb, let flesh retire;
   Speak through the earthquake, wind, and fire,
   O still, small voice of calm!

PRAYER
93
Have Thine Own Way, Lord!
ADELAIDE 5.4.5.4 D

Adelaide A. Pollard, 1902 George C. Stebbins, 1907

1. Have Thine own way, Lord! Have Thine own way! Thou art the Potter, I am the clay. Mold me and make me after Thy will, While I am waiting, yielded and still.

Have Thine Own Way, Lord!

1. Have Thine own way, Lord!
   Have Thine own way!
   Thou art the Potter, I am the clay.
   Mold me and make me after Thy will,
   While I am waiting, yielded and still.

2. Have Thine own way, Lord!
   Have Thine own way!
   Search me and try me, Savior, today!
   Wash me just now, Lord, wash me just now,
   As in Thy presence humbly I bow.

3. Have Thine own way, Lord!
   Have Thine own way!
   Wounded and weary, help me, I pray!
   Power, all power, surely is Thine!
   Touch me and heal me, Savior divine!

4. Have Thine own way, Lord!
   Have Thine own way!
   Hold o'er my being absolute sway!
   Fill with Thy Spirit till all shall see
   Christ only, always, living in me!

PRAYER

94 I Need Thee Every Hour

NEED   6.4.6.4 with refrain

Annie S. Hawks, 1872
Refrain added by Robert Lowry, 1872

Robert Lowry, 1872

1. I need Thee every hour, Most gracious Lord;
No tender voice like Thine Can peace afford.

Refrain
I need Thee, O I need Thee; Every hour I need Thee!
O bless me now, my Savior, I come to Thee!

I Need Thee Every Hour

PRAYER 94

1. I need Thee every hour, most gracious Lord;
   No tender voice like Thine can peace afford.
   > I need Thee, O I need Thee;
   > Every hour I need Thee!
   > O bless me now, my Savior,
   > I come to Thee!

2. I need Thee every hour; stay Thou nearby;
   Temptations lose their power when Thou art nigh.
   > I need Thee, O I need Thee;
   > Every hour I need Thee!
   > O bless me now, my Savior,
   > I come to Thee!

3. I need Thee every hour, in joy or pain;
   Come quickly and abide, or life is vain.
   > I need Thee, O I need Thee;
   > Every hour I need Thee!
   > O bless me now, my Savior,
   > I come to Thee!

4. I need Thee every hour, most Holy One;
   O make me Thine indeed, Thou blessed Son.
   > I need Thee, O I need Thee;
   > Every hour I need Thee!
   > O bless me now, my Savior,
   > I come to Thee!

PRAYER

95 In the Hour of Trial

PENITENCE 6.5.6.5 D

James Montgomery, 1834

Spencer Lane, 1879

1. In the hour of tri - al, Je - sus, plead for me,
Lest by base de - ni - al I de - part from Thee;
When Thou seest me wa - ver, With a look re - call,
Nor for fear or fa - vor Suf - fer me to fall.

In the Hour of Trial

1. In the hour of trial,
   Jesus, plead for me,
   Lest by base denial
   I depart from Thee;
   When Thou seest me waver,
   With a look recall,
   Nor for fear or favor
   Suffer me to fall.

2. With its witching pleasures
   Would this vain world charm,
   Or its sordid treasures
   Spread to work me harm,
   Bring to my remembrance
   Sad Gethsemane,
   Or, in darker semblance,
   Cross-crowned Calvary.

3. When in dust and ashes
   To the grave I sink,
   While heaven's glory flashes
   O'er the shelving brink,
   On Thy truth relying
   Through that mortal strife,
   Lord, receive me, dying,
   To eternal life.

PRAYER
96
Jesus, Lover of My Soul
MARTYN 7.7.7.7 D

Charles Wesley, 1740 — Simeon B. Marsh, 1834

1. Jesus, lover of my soul, Let me to Thy bosom fly,
While the nearer waters roll, While the tempest still is high:
Hide me, O my Savior, hide, Till the storm of life is past;
Safe into the haven guide; O receive my soul at last!

Jesus, Lover of My Soul

1. Jesus, lover of my soul,
   Let me to Thy bosom fly,
   While the nearer waters roll,
   While the tempest still is high:
   Hide me, O my Savior, hide,
   Till the storm of life is past;
   Safe into the haven guide;
   O receive my soul at last!

2. Other refuge have I none;
   Hangs my helpless soul on Thee;
   Leave, ah! leave me not alone,
   Still support and comfort me.
   All my trust on Thee is stayed,
   All my help from Thee I bring;
   Cover my defenseless head
   With the shadow of Thy wing.

3. Thou, O Christ, art all I want;
   More than all in Thee I find:
   Raise the fallen, cheer the faint,
   Heal the sick, and lead the blind.
   Just and holy is Thy name;
   I am all unrighteousness;
   False and full of sin I am,
   Thou art full of truth and grace.

PRAYER

97 Nearer, My God, to Thee

BETHANY   6.4.6.4.6.6.6.4

Sarah F. Adams, 1841   Lowell Mason, 1856

1. Nearer, my God, to Thee, Nearer to Thee!
E'en though it be a cross That raiseth me;
Still all my song shall be, Nearer, my God, to Thee,
Nearer, my God, to Thee, Nearer to Thee!

Nearer, My God, to Thee

1. Nearer, my God, to Thee,
   Nearer to Thee!
   E'en though it be a cross
   That raiseth me;
   Still all my song shall be,
   Nearer, my God, to Thee,
   Nearer, my God, to Thee,
   Nearer to Thee!

2. Though like the wanderer,
   The sun gone down,
   Darkness be over me,
   My rest a stone;
   Still in my dreams I'd be
   Nearer, my God, to Thee,
   Nearer, my God, to Thee,
   Nearer to Thee!

3. Then, with my waking thoughts
   Bright with Thy praise,
   Out of my stony griefs
   Bethel I'll raise;
   So by my woes to be
   Nearer, my God, to Thee,
   Nearer, my God, to Thee,
   Nearer to Thee!

PRAYER
98
Open My Eyes, That I May See

OPEN MY EYES 8.8.9.8 with refrain

Clara H. Scott, 1895   Clara H. Scott, 1895

1. O-pen my eyes, that I may see Glimps-es of truth Thou hast for me;
Place in my hands the won-der-ful key That shall un-clasp and set me free.

Refrain
Si-lent-ly now I wait for Thee, Read-y, my God, Thy will to see;
O-pen my eyes, il-lu-mine me, Spir-it di-vine!

Open My Eyes, That I May See

PRAYER 98

1. Open my eyes, that I may see
   Glimpses of truth Thou hast for me;
   Place in my hands the wonderful key
   That shall unclasp and set me free.
      Silently now I wait for Thee,
      Ready, my God, Thy will to see;
      Open my eyes, illumine me,
      Spirit divine!

2. Open my ears, that I may hear
   Voices of truth Thou sendest clear;
   And while the wave notes fall on my ear,
   Everything false will disappear.
      Silently now I wait for Thee,
      Ready, my God, Thy will to see;
      Open my ears, illumine me,
      Spirit divine!

3. Open my mouth, and let me bear
   Gladly the warm truth everywhere;
   Open my heart, and let me prepare
   Love with Thy children thus to share.
      Silently now I wait for Thee,
      Ready, my God, Thy will to see;
      Open my heart, illumine me,
      Spirit divine!

PRAYER

99 More Love to Thee, O Christ

MORE LOVE TO THEE 6.4.6.4.6.6.4.4

Elizabeth Payson Prentiss, 1856 — William Howard Doane, 1870

1. More love to Thee, O Christ, More love to Thee! Hear Thou the prayer I make On bended knee. This is my earnest plea: More love, O Christ, to Thee, More love to Thee, More love to Thee!

More Love to Thee, O Christ

PRAYER 99

1. More love to Thee, O Christ,
   More love to Thee!
   Hear Thou the prayer I make
   On bended knee.
   This is my earnest plea:
   More love, O Christ, to Thee,
   More love to Thee,
   More love to Thee!

2. Once earthly joy I craved,
   Sought peace and rest;
   Now Thee alone I seek,
   Give what is best.
   This all my prayer shall be:
   More love, O Christ, to Thee,
   More love to Thee,
   More love to Thee!

3. Then shall my latest breath
   Whisper Thy praise;
   This be the parting cry
   My heart shall raise.
   This still its prayer shall be:
   More love, O Christ, to Thee,
   More love to Thee,
   More love to Thee!

PRAYER
100 Lord, Speak to Me, That I May Speak
CANONBURY LM

Frances Ridley Havergal, 1872

Robert Schumann, 1839

1. Lord, speak to me, that I may speak In living echoes of Thy tone; As Thou hast sought, so let me seek Thine erring children lost and lone.

Lord, Speak to Me, That I May Speak

PRAYER 100

1. Lord, speak to me, that I may speak
   In living echoes of Thy tone;
   As Thou hast sought, so let me seek
   Thine erring children lost and lone.

2. O lead me, Lord, that I may lead
   The wandering and the wavering feet;
   O feed me, Lord, that I may feed
   Thy hungering ones with manna sweet.

3. O teach me, Lord, that I may teach
   The precious things Thou dost impart;
   And wing my words, that they may reach
   The hidden depths of many a heart.

4. O fill me with Thy fullness, Lord,
   Until my very heart o'erflow
   In kindling thought and glowing word,
   Thy love to tell, Thy praise to show.

5. O use me, Lord, use even me,
   Just as Thou wilt, and when, and where;
   Until Thy blessed face I see,
   Thy rest, Thy joy, Thy glory share.

PRAYER

101 Break Thou the Bread of Life

BREAD OF LIFE   6.4.6.4 D

Mary Artesmesia Lathbury, 1877

William Fiske Sherwin, 1877

1. Break Thou the bread of life, Dear Lord, to me,
As Thou didst break the loaves Beside the sea;
Beyond the sacred page I seek Thee, Lord;
My spirit pants for Thee, O living Word!

Break Thou the Bread of Life

PRAYER 101

1. Break Thou the bread of life,
   Dear Lord, to me,
   As Thou didst break the loaves
   Beside the sea;
   Beyond the sacred page
   I seek Thee, Lord;
   My spirit pants for Thee,
   O living Word!

2. Bless Thou the truth, dear Lord,
   Now unto me,
   As Thou didst bless the bread
   By Galilee;
   Then shall all bondage cease,
   All fetters fall;
   And I shall find my peace,
   My all in all.

PRAYER
102

Kum ba Yah
8.8.8.5

African-American spiritual   African melody

1. Kum ba yah, my Lord, kum ba yah! Kum ba yah, my Lord, kum ba yah! Kum ba yah, my Lord, kum ba yah! O Lord, kum ba yah!

Kum ba Yah

PRAYER 102

1. Kum ba yah,* my Lord, kum ba yah!
   Kum ba yah, my Lord, kum ba yah!
   Kum ba yah, my Lord, kum ba yah!
   O Lord, kum ba yah!

2. Someone's crying, Lord, kum ba yah!
   Someone's crying, Lord, kum ba yah!
   Someone's crying, Lord, kum ba yah!
   O Lord, kum ba yah!

3. Someone's singing, Lord, kum ba yah!
   Someone's singing, Lord, kum ba yah!
   Someone's singing, Lord, kum ba yah!
   O Lord, kum ba yah!

4. Someone's praying, Lord, kum ba yah!
   Someone's praying, Lord, kum ba yah!
   Someone's praying, Lord, kum ba yah!
   O Lord, kum ba yah!

* Come by here.

NATURE
103
This Is My Father's World
TERRA BEATA   SMD

Maltbie D. Babcock, 1901

Franklin L. Sheppard, 1915

1. This is my Father's world, And to my listening ears All nature sings, and 'round me rings The music of the spheres. This is my Father's world; I rest me in the thought Of rocks and trees, of skies and seas; His hand the wonders wrought.

This Is My Father's World

1. This is my Father's world,
   And to my listening ears
   All nature sings, and round me rings
   The music of the spheres.
   This is my Father's world;
   I rest me in the thought
   Of rocks and trees, of skies and seas;
   His hand the wonders wrought.

2. This is my Father's world,
   The birds their carols raise,
   The morning light, the lily white,
   Declare their Maker's praise.
   This is my Father's world:
   He shines in all that's fair;
   In the rustling grass I hear Him pass,
   He speaks to me everywhere.

3. This is my Father's world,
   Oh, let me ne'er forget
   That though the wrong seems oft so strong,
   God is the Ruler yet.
   This is my Father's world:
   The battle is not done;
   Jesus who died shall be satisfied,
   And earth and heaven be one.

NATURE
104

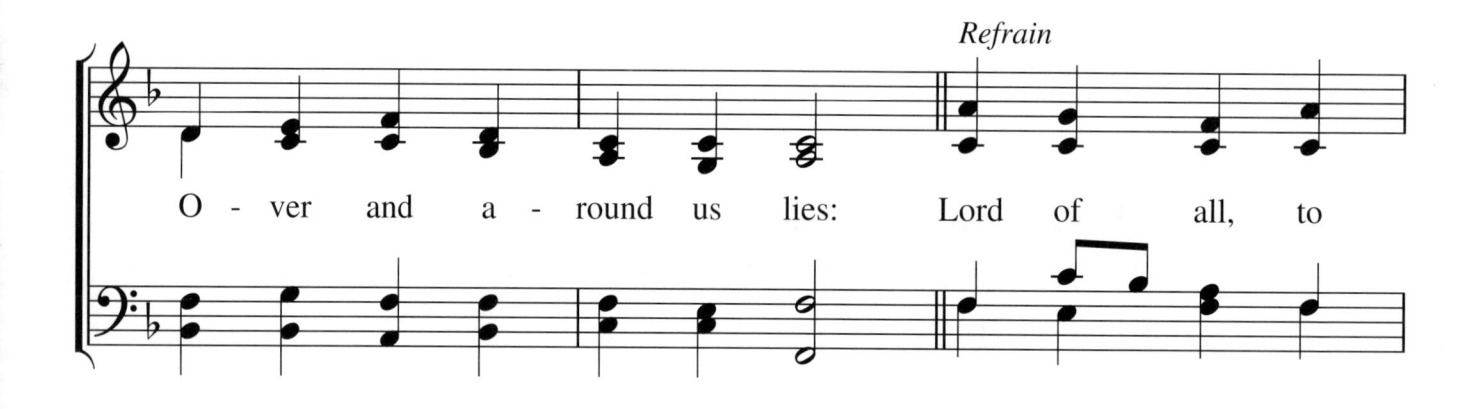

For the Beauty of the Earth

DIX 7.7.7.7.7.7

Folliott Sandford Pierpont, 1864

Conrad Kocher, 1838
Abr. William Henry Monk, 1861

1. For the beau-ty of the earth, For the glo-ry of the skies, For the love which from our birth Over and a-round us lies:

Refrain
Lord of all, to Thee we raise This our hymn of grate-ful praise.

For the Beauty of the Earth

1. For the beauty of the earth,
   For the glory of the skies,
   For the love which from our birth
   Over and around us lies:
      Lord of all, to Thee we raise
      This our hymn of grateful praise.

2. For the beauty of each hour
   Of the day and of the night,
   Hill and vale, and tree and flower,
   Sun and moon, and stars of light:
      Lord of all, to Thee we raise
      This our hymn of grateful praise.

3. For the joy of human love,
   Brother, sister, parent, child,
   Friends on earth, and friends above;
   For all gentle thoughts and mild:
      Lord of all, to Thee we raise
      This our hymn of grateful praise.

4. For Thy church, that evermore
   Lifteth holy hands above,
   Offering up on every shore
   Her pure sacrifice of love:
      Lord of all, to Thee we raise
      This our hymn of grateful praise.

NATURE
105

Fairest Lord Jesus
CRUSADERS' HYMN   5.6.8.5.5.8

Münster *Gesangbuch*, 1677
Trans. *Church Chorals and Choir Studies,* 1850; alt.

Silesian folk melody
In *Schlesische Volkslieder,* 1842

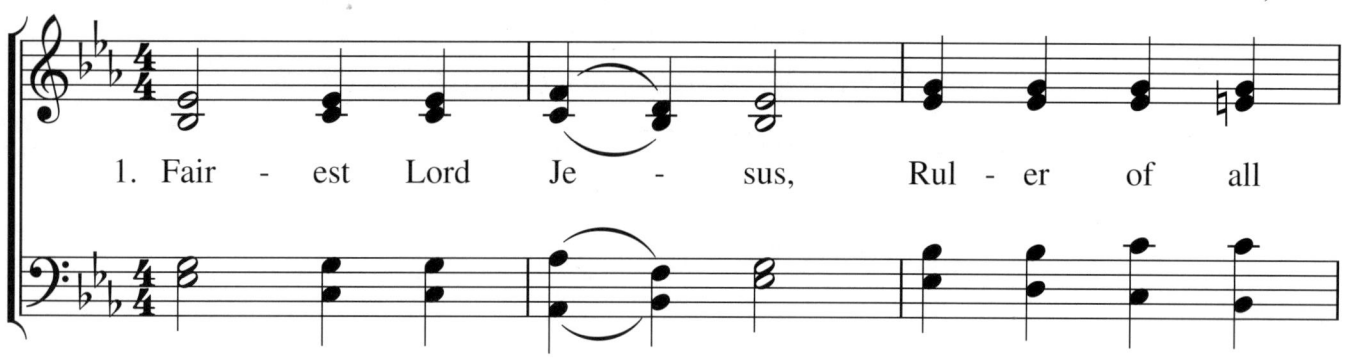

1. Fair-est Lord Je-sus, Rul-er of all na-ture, O Thou of God and man the Son, Thee will I cher-ish, Thee will I hon-or, Thou, my soul's glo-ry, joy, and crown.

Fairest Lord Jesus

NATURE
105

1. Fairest Lord Jesus,
   Ruler of all nature,
   O Thou of God and man the Son,
   Thee will I cherish,
   Thee will I honor,
   Thou, my soul's glory, joy, and crown.

2. Fair are the meadows,
   Fairer still the woodlands,
   Robed in the blooming garb of spring:
   Jesus is fairer,
   Jesus is purer,
   Who makes the woeful heart to sing.

3. Fair is the sunshine,
   Fairer still the moonlight,
   And all the twinkling, starry host:
   Jesus shines brighter,
   Jesus shines purer,
   Than all the angels heaven can boast.

FELLOWSHIP
106
The Church's One Foundation
AURELIA 7.6.7.6 D

Samuel John Stone, 1886 — Samuel Sebastian Wesley, 1864

1. The church's one foundation Is Jesus Christ her Lord; She is His new creation, By water and the word; From heaven He came and sought her To be His holy bride; With His own blood He bought her, And for her life He died.

The Church's One Foundation

1. The church's one foundation
   Is Jesus Christ her Lord;
   She is His new creation,
   By water and the word;
   From heaven He came and sought her
   To be His holy bride;
   With His own blood He bought her,
   And for her life He died.

2. Elect from every nation,
   Yet one o'er all the earth,
   Her charter of salvation
   One Lord, one faith, one birth;
   One holy name she blesses,
   Partakes one holy food,
   And to one hope she presses,
   With every grace endued.

3. Yet she on earth has union
   With God the Three in One,
   And mystic sweet communion
   With those whose rest is won:
   O happy ones and holy!
   Lord, give us grace that we,
   Like them, the meek and lowly,
   May live eternally.

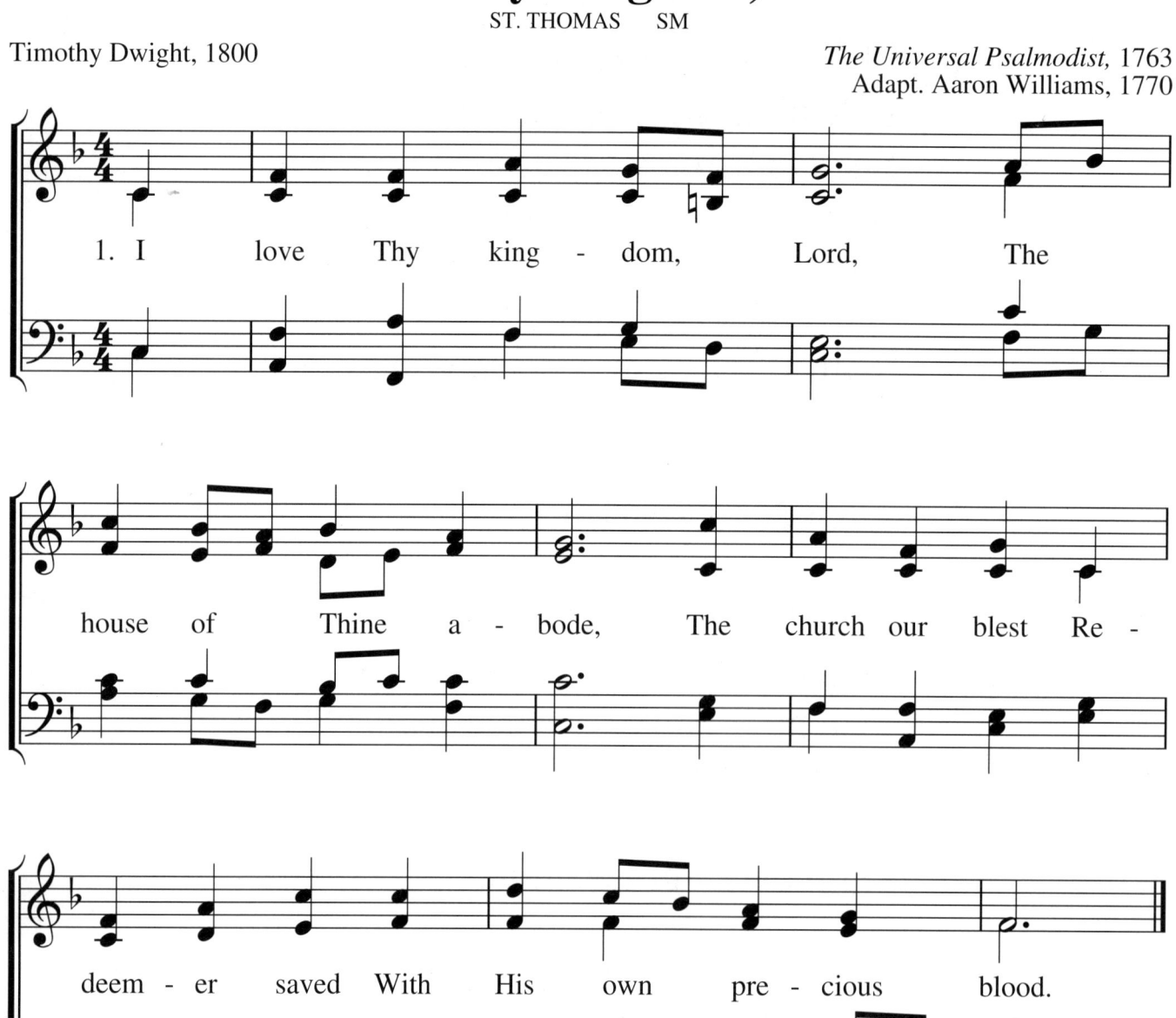

FELLOWSHIP
107 I Love Thy Kingdom, Lord
ST. THOMAS SM

Timothy Dwight, 1800

The Universal Psalmodist, 1763
Adapt. Aaron Williams, 1770

1. I love Thy kingdom, Lord, The house of Thine abode, The church our blest Redeemer saved With His own precious blood.

I Love Thy Kingdom, Lord

1. I love Thy kingdom, Lord,
   The house of Thine abode,
   The church our blest Redeemer saved
   With His own precious blood.

2. I love Thy church, O God;
   Her walls before Thee stand,
   Dear as the apple of Thine eye,
   And graven on Thy hand.

3. For her my tears shall fall,
   For her my prayers ascend;
   To her my cares and toils be given,
   Till toils and cares shall end.

4. Beyond my highest joy
   I prize her heavenly ways,
   Her sweet communion, solemn vows,
   Her hymns of love and praise.

5. Sure as Thy truth shall last,
   To Zion shall be given
   The brightest glories earth can yield,
   And brighter bliss of heaven.

FELLOWSHIP
108 Glorious Things of Thee Are Spoken
AUSTRIAN HYMN 8.7.8.7 D

John Newton, 1779; alt.   Franz Joseph Haydn, 1797

1. Glorious things of thee are spoken, Zion, city of our God;
God, whose word cannot be broken, Formed thee for a blest abode.
On the Rock of Ages founded, What can shake thy sure repose?
With salvation's walls surrounded, Thou may'st smile at all thy foes.

Glorious Things of Thee Are Spoken

1. Glorious things of thee are spoken,
   Zion, city of our God;
   God, whose word cannot be broken,
   Formed thee for a blest abode.
   On the Rock of Ages founded,
   What can shake thy sure repose?
   With salvation's walls surrounded,
   Thou may'st smile at all thy foes.

2. See, the streams of living waters,
   Springing from eternal love,
   Well supply thy sons and daughters,
   And all fear of want remove.
   Who can faint while such a river
   Ever flows their thirst to assuage?
   Grace, which like the Lord the giver,
   Never fails from age to age.

3. Round each habitation hovering,
   See the cloud and fire appear
   For a glory and a covering,
   Showing that the Lord is near.
   Thus deriving from their banner
   Light by night and shade by day,
   Safe they feed upon the manna
   Which God gives them when they pray.

FELLOWSHIP

109 Blest Be the Tie That Binds

DENNIS SM

John Fawcett, 1782

Johann Georg Nägeli, 1773–1836
Arr. Lowell Mason, 1845

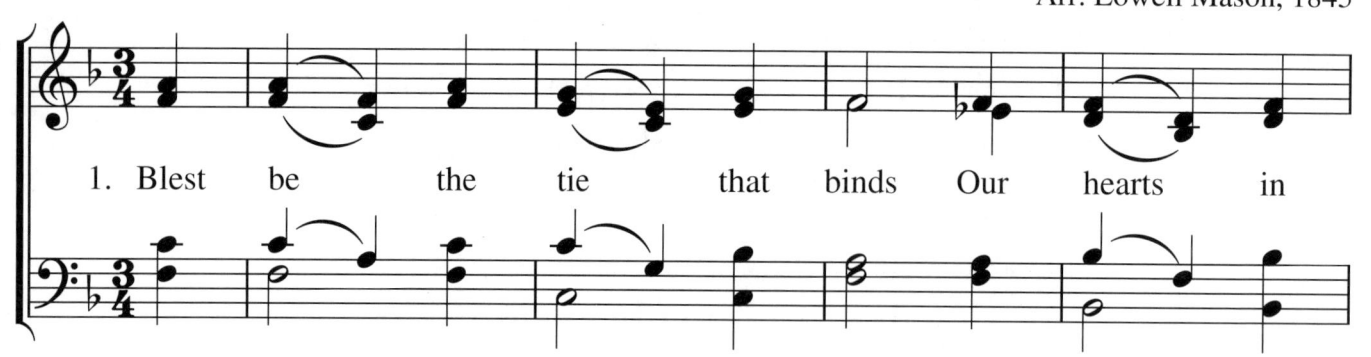

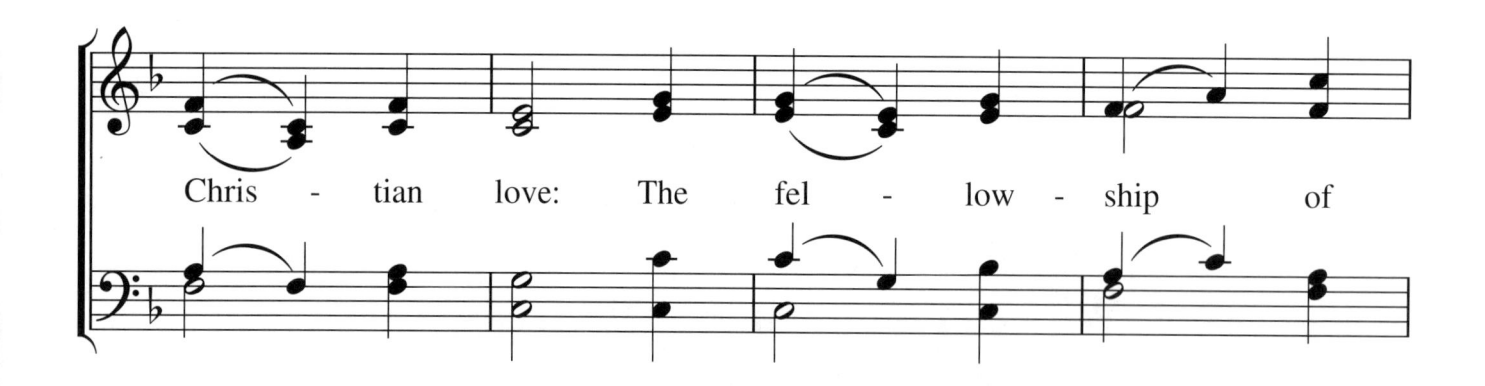

1. Blest be the tie that binds Our hearts in Christian love: The fellowship of kindred minds Is like to that above.

Blest Be the Tie That Binds

1. Blest be the tie that binds
   Our hearts in Christian love:
   The fellowship of kindred minds
   Is like to that above.

2. Before our Father's throne
   We pour our ardent prayers;
   Our fears, our hopes, our aims are one,
   Our comforts and our cares.

3. We share our mutual woes,
   Our mutual burdens bear,
   And often for each other flows
   The sympathizing tear.

4. From sorrow, toil, and pain,
   And sin we shall be free;
   And perfect love and friendship reign
   Through all eternity.

MISSION
110
Christ for the World We Sing!

ITALIAN HYMN 6.6.4.6.6.6.4

Samuel Wolcott, 1869   Felice de Giardini, 1769

1. Christ for the world we sing! The world to Christ we bring With loving zeal; The poor, and them that mourn, The faint and o-ver-borne, Sin-sick and sor-row-worn, Whom Christ doth heal.

Christ for the World We Sing!

MISSION 110

1. Christ for the world we sing!
   The world to Christ we bring
   With loving zeal;
   The poor, and them that mourn,
   The faint and overborne,
   Sinsick and sorrow-worn,
   Whom Christ doth heal.

2. Christ for the world we sing;
   The world to Christ we bring
   With fervent prayer;
   The wayward and the lost,
   By restless passions tossed,
   Redeemed at countless cost
   From dark despair.

3. Christ for the world we sing;
   The world to Christ we bring
   With joyful song;
   The newborn souls whose days,
   Reclaimed from error's ways,
   Inspired with hope and praise,
   To Christ belong.

MISSION

111 Christ Is Made the Sure Foundation

REGENT SQUARE   8.7.8.7.8.7

Latin (7th century)
Trans. John Mason Neale, 1851

Henry Thomas Smart, 1867

1. Christ is made the sure foun-da-tion, Christ the head and cor-ner-stone, Cho-sen of the Lord and pre-cious, Bind-ing all the church in one; Ho-ly Zi-on's help for-ev-er, And our con-fi-dence a-lone.

Christ Is Made the Sure Foundation

MISSION 111

1. Christ is made the sure foundation,
   Christ the head and cornerstone,
   Chosen of the Lord and precious,
   Binding all the church in one;
   Holy Zion's help forever,
   And our confidence alone.

2. To this temple, where we call Thee,
   Come, O Lord of hosts, today:
   With Thy wonted lovingkindness
   Hear Thy people as they pray;
   And Thy fullest benediction
   Shed within its walls alway.

3. Laud and honor to the Father,
   Laud and honor to the Son,
   Laud and honor to the Spirit,
   Ever Three and ever One,
   One in might, and One in glory,
   While unending ages run!

MISSION

112 Jesus Shall Reign Where'er the Sun

DUKE STREET   LM

Isaac Watts, 1719; alt.   John Hatton, 1793

1. Je - sus shall reign wher - e'er the sun
Does its suc - ces - sive jour - neys run;
His king - dom spread from shore to shore,
Till moons shall wax and wane no more.

Jesus Shall Reign Where'er the Sun

1. Jesus shall reign where'er the sun
   Does its successive journeys run;
   His kingdom spread from shore to shore,
   Till moons shall wax and wane no more.

2. To Him shall endless prayer be made,
   And praises throng to crown His head;
   His name, like sweet perfume, shall rise
   With every morning sacrifice.

3. People and realms of every tongue
   Dwell on His love with sweetest song,
   And infant voices shall proclaim
   Their early blessings on His name.

4. Blessings abound where'er He reigns;
   The prisoners leap to lose their chains,
   The weary find eternal rest,
   And all who suffer want are blest.

5. Let every creature rise and bring
   Honors peculiar to our King;
   Angels descend with songs again,
   And earth repeat the loud Amen!

THANKSGIVING
113 Come, Ye Thankful People, Come
ST. GEORGE'S WINDSOR 7.7.7.7 D

Henry Alford, 1844   George Job Elvey, 1859

1. Come, ye thankful people, come, Raise the song of harvest home:
All is safely gathered in, Ere the winter storms begin;
God, our Maker, doth provide For our wants to be supplied:
Come to God's own temple, come, Raise the song of harvest home.

Come, Ye Thankful People, Come

THANKSGIVING 113

1. Come, ye thankful people, come,
   Raise the song of harvest home:
   All is safely gathered in,
   Ere the winter storms begin;
   God, our Maker, doth provide
   For our wants to be supplied:
   Come to God's own temple, come,
   Raise the song of harvest home.

2. All the world is God's own field,
   Fruit unto his praise to yield;
   Wheat and tares together sown,
   Unto joy and sorrow grown;
   First the blade, and then the ear,
   Then the full corn shall appear:
   Lord of harvest, grant that we
   Wholesome grain and pure may be.

3. Even so, Lord, quickly come
   To Thy final harvest home;
   Gather all Thy people in,
   Free from sorrow, free from sin;
   There, forever purified,
   In Thy presence to abide;
   Come, with all your angels, come,
   Raise the glorious harvest home.

THANKSGIVING
114
Now Thank We All Our God
NUN DANKET ALLE GOTT 6.7.6.7.6.6.6.6

Martin Rinkart, 1636
Trans. Catherine Winkworth, 1858; alt.
Stanza 3, *Rejoice in the Lord,* 1985

Johann Crüger, 1647
Harmony adapted from *Lobgesang,*
Felix Mendelssohn, 1840

1. Now thank we all our God With heart and hands and voic-es, Who won-drous things hath done, In whom this world re-joic-es; Who, from our moth-ers' arms, Hath blessed us on our way With count-less gifts of love, And still is ours to-day.

Now Thank We All Our God

1. Now thank we all our God
   With heart and hands and voices,
   Who wondrous things hath done,
   In whom this world rejoices;
   Who, from our mothers' arms,
   Hath blessed us on our way
   With countless gifts of love,
   And still is ours today.

2. O may this bounteous God
   Through all our life be near us,
   With ever-joyful hearts
   And blessed peace to cheer us;
   And keep us in God's grace,
   And guide us when perplexed,
   And free us from all ills
   In this world and the next.

3. All praise and thanks to God,
   Who reigns in highest heaven,
   To Father and to Son
   And Spirit now be given,
   The one eternal God,
   Whom heaven and earth adore,
   The God who was, and is,
   And shall be evermore.

THANKSGIVING

115 We Gather Together

KREMSER   12.11.12.11

Netherlands folk hymn
Trans. Theodore Baker, 1894

Nederlandtsch Gedenckclanck, 1626
Harm. Edward Kremser, 1877

1. We gather together to ask the Lord's blessing; He chastens and hastens His will to make known; The wicked oppressing now cease from distressing, Sing praises to His name; He forgets not His own.

We Gather Together

1. We gather together to ask the Lord's blessing;
   He chastens and hastens His will to make known;
   The wicked oppressing now cease from distressing,
   Sing praises to His name; He forgets not His own.

2. Beside us to guide us, our God with us joining,
   Ordaining, maintaining His kingdom divine;
   So from the beginning the fight we were winning;
   Thou, Lord, wast at our side; All glory be Thine!

3. We all do extol Thee, Thou leader triumphant,
   And pray that Thou still our defender wilt be.
   Let Thy congregation escape tribulation;
   Thy name be ever praised! O Lord, make us free!

THE NATION
116
My Country, 'Tis of Thee
AMERICA 6.6.4.6.6.6.4

Samuel Francis Smith, 1831

Thesaurus Musicus, c. 1740

1. My country, 'tis of thee, Sweet land of liberty, Of thee I sing; Land where my fathers died, Land of the pilgrims' pride, From every mountainside Let freedom ring.

My Country, 'Tis of Thee

THE NATION 116

1. My country, 'tis of thee,
   Sweet land of liberty,
   Of thee I sing;
   Land where my fathers died,
   Land of the pilgrims' pride,
   From every mountainside
   Let freedom ring.

2. My native country, thee,
   Land of the noble free,
   Thy name I love;
   I love thy rocks and rills,
   Thy woods and templed hills;
   My heart with rapture thrills
   Like that above.

3. Our fathers' God, to Thee,
   Author of liberty,
   To Thee we sing:
   Long may our land be bright
   With freedom's holy light;
   Protect us by Thy might,
   Great God, our King.

THE NATION

117 O Beautiful for Spacious Skies

MATERNA CMD

Katharine Lee Bates, 1893

Samuel Augustus Ward, 1882

1. O beau-ti-ful for spa-cious skies, For am-ber waves of grain, For pur-ple moun-tain maj-es-ties A-bove the fruit-ed plain! A-mer-i-ca! A-mer-i-ca! God shed His grace on thee, And crown thy good with broth-er-hood From sea to shin-ing sea!

O Beautiful for Spacious Skies

1. O beautiful for spacious skies,
   For amber waves of grain,
   For purple mountain majesties
   Above the fruited plain!
   America! America!
   God shed His grace on thee,
   And crown thy good with brotherhood
   From sea to shining sea!

2. O beautiful for pilgrim feet,
   Whose stern, impassioned stress
   A thoroughfare for freedom beat
   Across the wilderness!
   America! America!
   God mend thine every flaw,
   Confirm thy soul in self-control,
   Thy liberty in law!

3. O beautiful for patriot dream
   That sees beyond the years
   Thine alabaster cities gleam,
   Undimmed by human tears!
   America! America!
   God shed His grace on thee
   And crown thy good with brotherhood
   From sea to shining sea!

THE NATION

118 Eternal Father, Strong to Save

MELITA 8.8.8.8.8.8

William Whiting, 1860

John Bacchus Dykes, 1861

1. E-ter-nal Fa-ther, strong to save, Whose arm has bound the rest-less wave, Who bade the might-y o-cean deep Its own ap-point-ed lim-its keep: O hear us when we cry to Thee For those in per-il on the sea.

Eternal Father, Strong to Save

1. Eternal Father, strong to save,
   Whose arm has bound the restless wave,
   Who bade the mighty ocean deep
   Its own appointed limits keep:
   O hear us when we cry to Thee
   For those in peril on the sea.

2. O Savior, whose almighty word
   The wind and waves submissive heard,
   Who walked upon the foaming deep,
   And calm amid its rage did sleep:
   O hear us when we cry to Thee
   For those in peril on the sea.

3. O Holy Spirit, who did brood
   Upon the chaos wild and rude,
   And bade its angry tumult cease,
   And gave, for fierce confusion, peace:
   O hear us when we cry to Thee
   For those in peril on the sea.

4. O Trinity of love and power,
   All travelers guard in danger's hour;
   From rock and tempest, fire and foe,
   Protect them wheresoe'er they go;
   Thus evermore shall rise to Thee
   Glad praise from air and land and sea.

WORSHIP AIDS

119 Praise God from Whom All Blessings Flow

OLD HUNDREDTH   LM

Thomas Ken, 1695, 1709

Genevan Psalter, 1551

Praise God from whom all bless-ings flow; Praise Him, all crea-tures here be-low; Praise Him a-bove, ye heaven-ly host; Praise Fa-ther, Son, and Ho-ly Ghost. A-men.

120 Gloria Patri

Henry W. Greatorex, 1851

Glo-ry be to the Fa-ther, and to the Son, and to the Ho-ly Ghost; As it was in the be-gin-ning, is now, and ev-er shall be, world with-out end. A-men, A-men.

Praise God from Whom All Blessings Flow 119

Praise God from whom all blessings flow;
Praise Him, all creatures here below;
Praise Him above, ye heavenly host;
Praise Father, Son, and Holy Ghost. Amen.

Gloria Patri 120

Glory be to the Father,
and to the Son,
and to the Holy Ghost;

As it was in the beginning,
is now, and ever shall be,
world without end.
Amen, Amen.

The Apostles' Creed

I believe in God the Father Almighty,
   Maker of heaven and earth,

And in Jesus Christ his only Son our Lord;
   who was conceived by the Holy Ghost,
   born of the Virgin Mary,
   suffered under Pontius Pilate,
   was crucified, dead, and buried;
   he descended into hell;
   the third day he rose again from the dead;
   he ascended into heaven, and sitteth on the
     right hand of God the Father Almighty;
   from thence he shall come to judge the
     quick and the dead.

I believe in the Holy Ghost;
   the holy catholic church;
   the communion of saints;
   the forgiveness of sins;
   the resurrection of the body;
   and the life everlasting.   Amen.

The Lord's Prayer

Our Father who art in heaven,
   hallowed be Thy name.
Thy kingdom come,
Thy will be done,
   on earth as it is in heaven.
Give us this day our daily bread;
and forgive us our debts,*
   as we forgive our debtors;**
and lead us not into temptation,
   but deliver us from evil.
For Thine is the kingdom,
   and the power,
   and the glory, forever.   Amen.

* *Or* our trespasses,
** *Or* those who trespass against us;

Alphabetical Index of Tunes

Adelaide 93
Adeste fideles 34
Amazing Grace 61
America 116
Angel's Story 89
Antioch 43
Assurance 63
Aurelia 106
Austrian Hymn 108
Azmon 11

Beecher 72
Bethany 97
Bradbury 77
Bread of Life 101

Canonbury 100
Carol 40
Chautauqua (*see* Evening Praise)
Christmas 42
Converse 65
Coronation 8
Crusaders' Hymn 105
Cwm Rhondda 81

Dalehurst 79
Darwall's 148th 10
Dennis 109
Diademata 13

Dix 44, 104
Duke Street 112

Easter Hymn 53
Ein' feste Burg 15
Ellers 23
Eucharistic Hymn 29
Evan 3
Evening Praise 19
Eventide 21

Foundation 85

Galilee 60
Germany 90
Greensleeves 37

Hamburg 49
Hankey (*see* I Love to Tell the Story)
Hanover 12
Hendon 86
He Leadeth Me 64
Hursley 20
Hyfrydol 31
Hymn to Joy 4

I Love to Tell the Story 66
In Babilone 88
I Want to Be a Christian 84
Italian Hymn 7, 110

Jesus Loves Me 71

Kremser 115
Kum ba Yah 102

Lancashire 55, 82
Laudes Domini 16

ALPHABETICAL INDEX OF TUNES

Let Us Break Bread 28
Lobe den Herren 9
Lyons 6

Martyn 96
Maryton 83
Materna 117
McAfee 91
Melita 118
Mendelssohn 39
Mercy 58
Merrial 22
Morecambe 25, 59
More Love to Thee 99
Mueller 38

Need 94
Nettleton 78
Nicaea 5
Nun danket alle Gott 114

Old Hundredth 1, 119
Olivet 70
Open My Eyes 98

Passion Chorale 48
Penitence 95
Pilot 76

Quebec 26

Rathbun 50
Regent Square 111
Rest 92

St. Agnes 57, 80
St. Anne 2
St. Catherine 69

St. Christopher 52
St. Clement 18
St. Denio 14
St. Drostane 47
St. Flavian 27
St. George's Windsor 33, 113
St. Gertrude 68
St. Kevin 54
St. Louis 35
St. Margaret 74
St. Theodulph (*see* Valet will ich dir geben)
St. Thomas 107
Schumann 87
Scott (*see* Open My Eyes)
Serenity 73
Sicilian Mariners 24
Stille Nacht 36

Tallis' Canon 17
Terra beata 103
The First Nowell 41
Three Kings of Orient 45
Toplady 75
Trentham 56
Truro 32

Valet will ich dir geben 46
Veni Emmanuel 30

Warner (*see* Jesus Loves Me)
Webb 67
Were You There 51
Woodworth 62

Index of First Lines

A mighty fortress is our God 15
Abide with me 21
All glory, laud, and honor 46
All hail the power of Jesus' name 8
All people that on earth do dwell 1
All praise to Thee, my God, this night 17
Amazing grace 61
As with gladness men of old 44
Away in a manger 38
Be known to us in breaking bread 27
Beneath the cross of Jesus 52
Blessed assurance, Jesus is mine! 63
Blest be the tie that binds 109
Bread of the world 29
Break Thou the bread of life 101
Breathe on me, Breath of God 56
Christ for the world we sing 110
Christ is made the sure foundation 111
Come, Holy Spirit, heavenly Dove 57
Come, Thou Almighty King 7
Come, Thou Fount of every blessing 78
Come, Thou long-expected Jesus 31
Come, ye faithful, raise the strain 54
Come, ye thankful people, come 113
Crown Him with many crowns 13
Day is dying in the west 19
Dear Lord and Father of mankind 92
Eternal Father, strong to save 118
Fairest Lord Jesus 105

INDEX OF FIRST LINES

Faith of our fathers	69
For the beauty of the earth	104
Gloria Patri	120
Glory be to the Father	120
Glorious things of Thee are spoken	108
Guide me, O Thou great Jehovah	81
Hark! The herald angels sing	39
Have Thine own way, Lord	93
He leadeth me: O blessed thought!	64
Here, O my Lord, I see Thee face to face	25
Holy Spirit, truth divine	58
Holy, holy, holy! Lord God Almighty	5
How firm a foundation	85
I love Thy kingdom, Lord	107
I love to tell the story	66
I need Thee every hour	94
Immortal Love, forever full	73
In the cross of Christ I glory	50
In the hour of trial	95
It came upon the midnight clear	40
Jesus calls us	60
Jesus Christ is risen today	53
Jesus loves me!	71
Jesus shall reign where'er the sun	112
Jesus, lover of my soul	96
Jesus, Savior, pilot me	76
Jesus, the very thought of Thee	80
Jesus, Thou joy of loving hearts	26
Joy to the world!	43
Joyful, joyful, we adore Thee	4
Just as I am, without one plea	62
Kum ba yah	102
Lead on, O King eternal	82
Let us break bread together	28
Lift up your heads, ye mighty gates	32
Lord, dismiss us with Thy blessing	24
Lord, I want to be a Christian	84
Lord, speak to me that I may speak	100

INDEX OF FIRST LINES

Love divine, all loves excelling 72
More love to Thee, O Christ 99
My country, 'tis of thee 116
My faith looks up to Thee 70
Near to the heart of God 91
Nearer, my God, to Thee 97
Now thank we all our God 114
Now the day is over 22
O beautiful for spacious skies 117
O come, all ye faithful 34
O come, O come, Emmanuel 30
O for a closer walk with God 79
O for a thousand tongues to sing 11
O Jesus, I have promised 89
O little town of Bethlehem 35
O Love that wilt not let me go 74
O Master, let me walk with Thee 83
O sacred head, now wounded 48
O worship the King, all glorious above 6
Onward, Christian soldiers 68
Open my eyes that I may see 98
Our God, our help in ages past 2
Praise God from whom all blessings flow 119
Praise ye the Lord, the Almighty 9
Rejoice, the Lord is King 10
Ride on! Ride on in majesty 47
Rock of Ages, cleft for me 75
Savior, again to Thy dear name we raise 23
Savior, like a shepherd lead us 77
Silent night, holy night 36
Spirit of God, descend upon my heart 59
Stand up, stand up for Jesus 67
Sun of my soul, Thou Savior dear 20
Take my life 86
The church's one foundation 106
The day of resurrection 55
The day Thou gavest, Lord, is ended 18
The first Nowell 41

The Lord's my Shepherd, I'll not want	3
There is a place of quiet rest	91
There's a wideness in God's mercy	88
This is my Father's world	103
Watchman, tell us of the night	33
We gather together to ask the Lord's blessing	115
We give Thee but Thine own	87
We three kings of Orient are	45
Were you there?	51
What a friend we have in Jesus	65
What Child is this	37
When I survey the wondrous cross	49
When morning gilds the skies	16
Where cross the crowded ways of life	90
While shepherds watched their flocks	42
Ye servants of God, your Master proclaim	12